An American in Paris

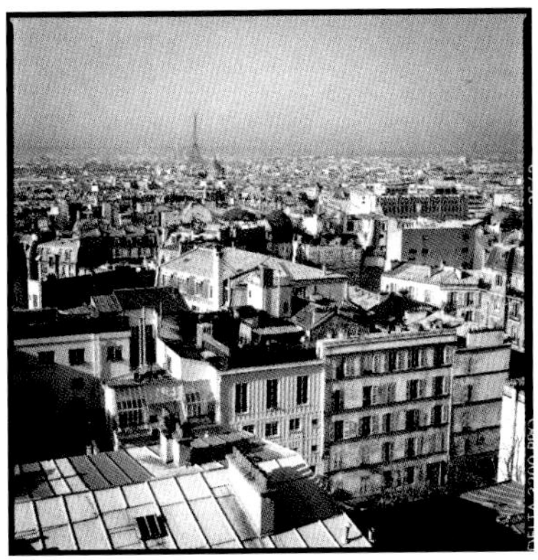

An American in Paris

The Cordial Traveler Inside Guide

Photographed by Véronique Vial

Text by Nadia Hamam

Preface and Translation
by Nicolas Duchemin Harvard

Edited by Ly VoDoan

RPM

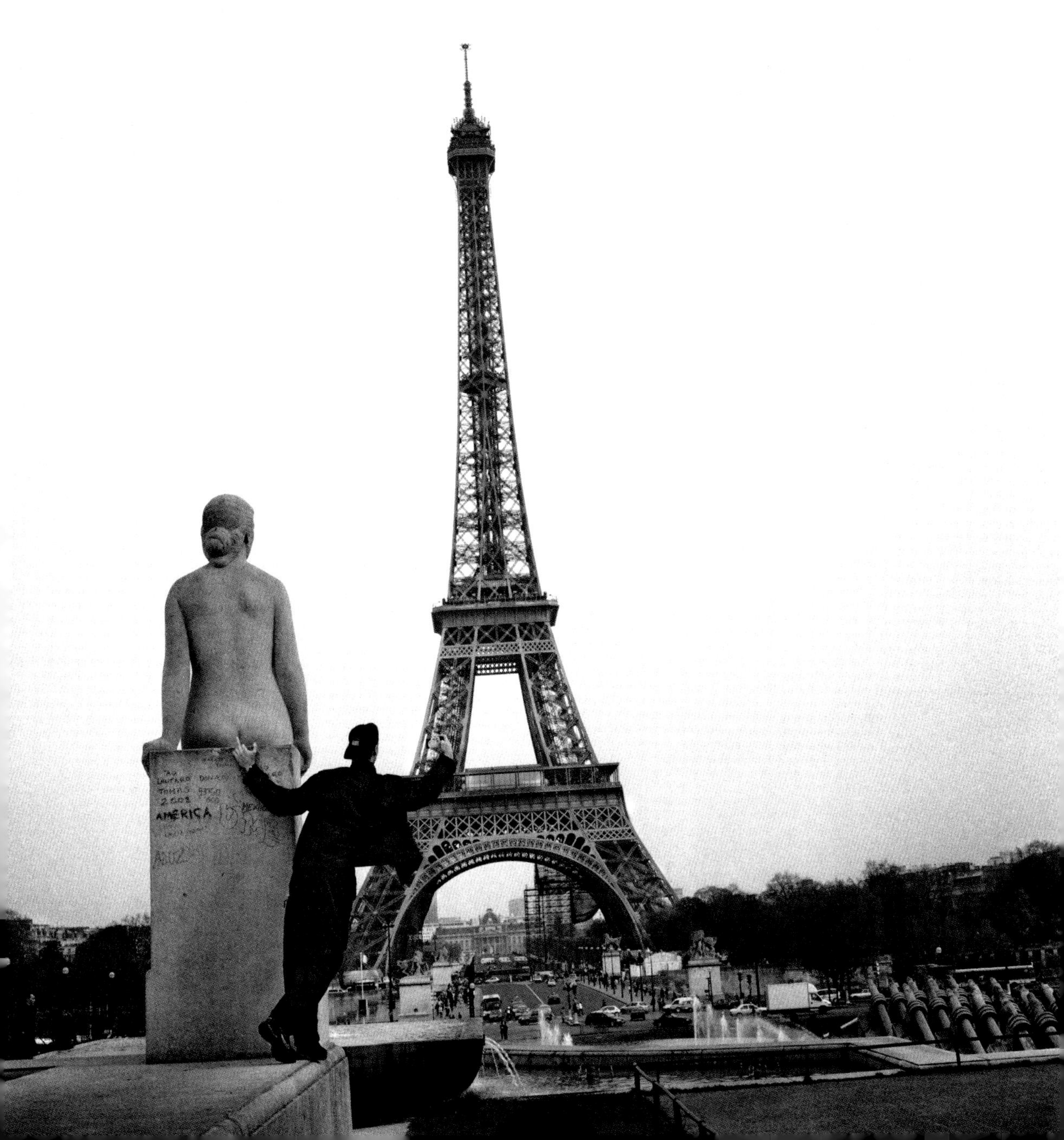
AMERICA

content

Bonjour!

Welcome to Paris, one of the most beautiful cities in the world, a city commonly famous for its gorgeous women, fine wine, smelly cheese... and yes, those berets. Visitors and residents alike cannot deny that the cathedrals, palaces, monuments, opera houses, theatres, hotels, residences, and even the various little squares that separate these buildings make Paris an exquisite collection of architecture that has long been praised by the rest of the world. There can never really be enough said about the architecture of Paris. Within the labyrinth of Haussmanian edifices, in a maze of large boulevards and narrow, winding streets, you will discover the many villages that make up Paris – Belleville, Montmartre, Montparnasse, le Seixieme, le Quartier Latin, Saint Germain des Pres, Bastille, Chatelet, Beaubourg, le Marais, le Sentier, and many others. In each village lives a different kind of Parisian, characterized by with different behavior, fashion sense, etiquettes, mentality, etc.

In this city of cobblestones and manicured parks dwell sophisticated urbanites who view their home from fine-living perspective. The Parisian lifestyle is more about wining and dining than it is about engulfing oneself in the rich culture of art and literature that is known to overwhelm tourists. Where do you start in a city so full of attractions and must-do's? Good question. This guide will attempt to take you, the American in Paris, on an adventure through Paris and exposing you to places favored by regular visitors, giving you a taste of delights enjoyed by the locals and showing you other hotspots that have been given the two thumbs up!

For you adventure-seeking Americans, we first suggest that you simply wander the streets, get a little lost, and on your way to nowhere specific you will discover the frenzy of the boulevards, the calmness of the parks and the madness of the crowded night-clubs. Sit at a smoky café and start a novel, drink cup after cup of short espressos. Don't forget to use the Metro, experience it's unmistakable smell, and let the train take you to a surprise destination. Check out retail stores and see if Paris trends agree with you. Catch a classic flick at an old theatre with rotting seats and no fire exits – go vintage chic all the way, baby! The alternative is to take your beloved to an opera at the Palais Garnier, followed by an expensive and delicious three-hour meal at the restaurant of their choice.

Food. Oh yes, we French have every right to proudly boast this part of our culture. Unanimously voted one of the finest cuisines on earth, French dining introduces you to a plethora of meat, seafood, vegetables, an array of delicate sauces and dressings that will spoil your palate and transform you into a food snob. No French meal is complete without an excellent bottle of wine or champagne, and your waiter will inevitably give you a thorough rundown of his wine list. Finish your meal with any French dessert. Whatever you choose, it will surely be even more delectable than your pronunciation of it was bad.

You can observe some interesting elements in the "loose morals" and sexual openness of the French prostitutes who will try to lure you with irresistible fervor. Or go see any of the eye-opening shows in the Pigalle district. In bars and clubs as well as in the streets, take pleasure in the provocative long stares and smiles for what they really mean. You might find a second or even third party to indulge you in your most powerful fantasies. Remember that you can also take the whole party back to your honeymoon suite at any of the city's sexy hotels. Lone travelers shouldn't feel shy about hooking up – walk up to someone sitting on a park bench reading a book, tell them how much you want to make love to them. Who would better understand this kind of sexual directness than a Parisian? After a night of intense passion in their studio apartment, say Adieu with the same passionate honesty. Have a divine breakfast in a nearby brasserie, where insults await you from your serving waiter, insults that would sound like Cyrano de Bergerac poetry breezing through the warm mid-morning air.

A thousand poets could write about Paris for another thousand years but none would fully capture the essence of living there, as words could never do justice. What we hope to provide in this little book are addresses, brief descriptions and important information to guide you on your journey through the bejeweled city of love, fashion, stylish hotels, fine dining, endless nightlife and entertainment, sex, music, art, literature, and so many other beautiful things... Ultimately, this guide aims to help you experience Paris like a Parisian. Live and love in the City of Lights, do it one day at a time if you prefer, but live it fully. Enjoy!

best bistros

A full stomach gives confidence.

Fench proverb, from Auvergne

Le Clos St Honoré

For a savory dinner in a tastefully renovated 17th century cellar.

3, rue Saint Hyacinthe, 75001 Paris
Tel: 01 40 15 09 36

L'Auvergne Gourmande

A welcoming table d'hôte, offering an elaborate cuisine made of appetizing ingredients, accompanied by excellent wines.

127, rue St Dominique 75007 Paris
Tel: 01 47 05 60 79

Le Chateaubriand

The 1930s decor is simple but elegant.

129, avenue Parmentier, 75011 Paris
Tel: 01 43 57 45 95

Chez Ramulaud

Tasty and nutritious food in a family setting.

269, rue du Faubourg St Antoine, 75011 Paris
Tel: 01 43 72 23 29

Beurre Noisette

A great place if your're looking for fresh food from the day's market.

68, rue Vasco de Gama, 75015 Paris
Tel: 01 48 56 82 49

Le Brespail

Here you'll discover the origins of Basque and Landes cuisine.

159, rue du Faubourg St Antoine, 75011 Paris
Tel: 01 43 41 99 13

best bistros

An empty stomach is also deaf.

Fench proverb.

Autour du Mont

For a gastronomic visit to Normandy.

58, rue Vasco de Gama, 75015 Paris
Tel: 01 42 50 55 63

Comme Cochon

Pork, a lot of pork.

135, rue de Charenton, 75012 Paris
Tel: 01 43 42 43 36

A mi chemin

A simple setting brings your attention back to the food.

31, rue Boulard, 75014 Paris
Tel: 01 45 39 56 45

L'homme Bleu Rest Berbere

The decor sends you on an express trip to the Sahara.

55 bis rue Jean Pierre Timbeau, 75011 Paris
Tel: 01 48 07 05 63

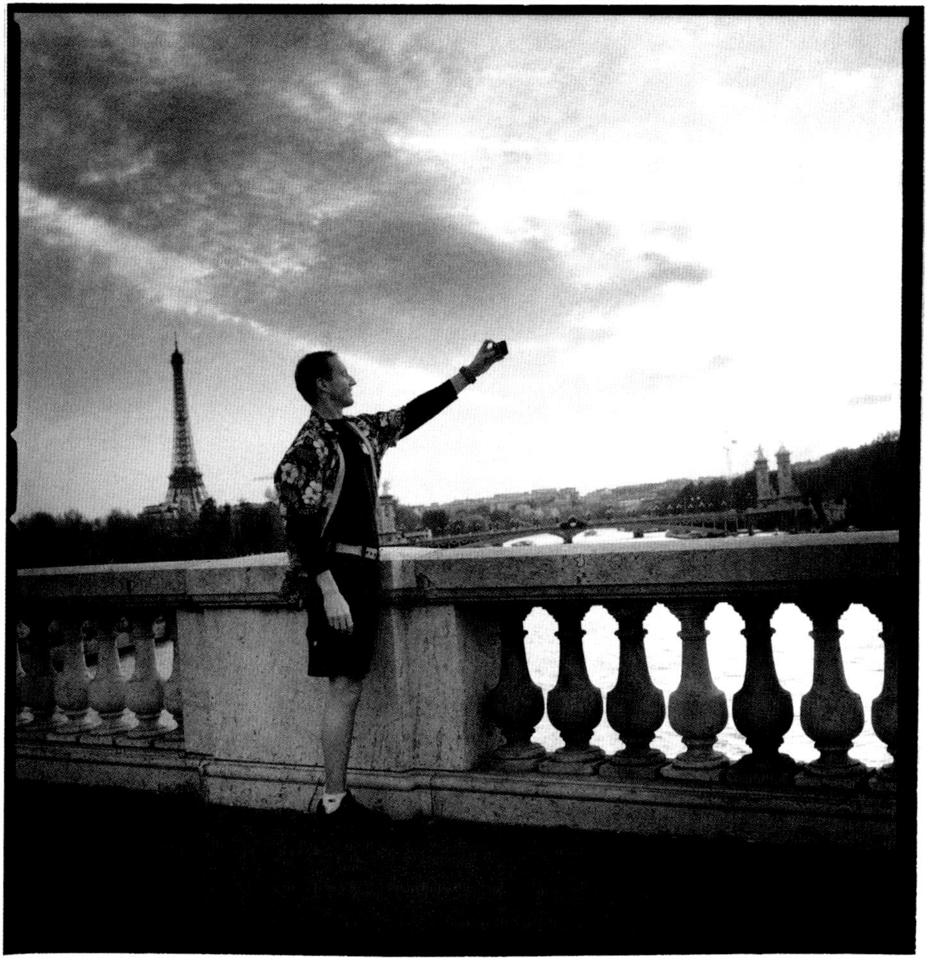

Have proof that you were there ...
not just the 10 lbs you gained from the food.

A dish of pike is more effective than a letter of recommendation.

La vingt cinquième image

Trendy place in a trendy neighborhood, this restaurant is built in the walls of an old bakery in the
Belle Epoque style.

9, rue des Récollets, 75010 Paris
Tel: 01 40 35 80 88

Les Cailloux

An excellent Italian deli, styled by New York loft architecture.

58, rue des Cinq Diamants, 75013 Paris
Tel: 01 45 80 15 08

tables that serve after 11pm

China Club

This little jewel exudes a 1930s Shanghai ambiance, serves delicate Chinese dinners 30 euros until 12:30 am.

50 rue de Charenton 75012 Paris
Tel: 01 43 43 82 02

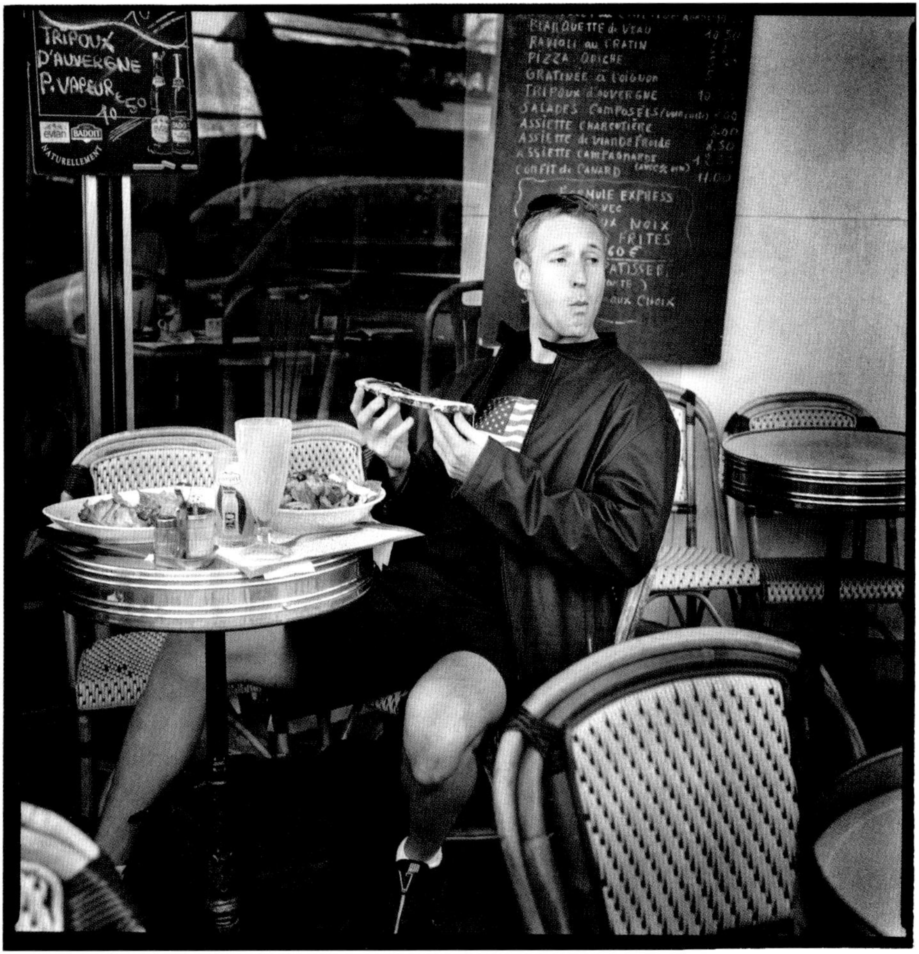

Wow! Even French fast food is gourmet.

Always well is one who dances.

Fench proverb

Le Georges

Until 2 am, the Georges Pompidou Center's trendy restaurant serves a delicious cuisine to be savored as you gaze at one of the most breath-taking views in Paris.

Centre Georges Pompidou
19, rue Beaubourg 75004 Paris
Tel: 01 44 78 47 99

Vin et Marée

Until midnight, enjoy the best fish of irreproachable freshness and quality.

108, avenue du Maine 75014 Paris
Tel: 01 43 20 29 50

Les Editeurs

Until 2am, in the heart of St. Germain des Prés, you can have a simple a la carte meal for 30 euros in a library setting.

4, carrefour de l'Odéon. 75006 Paris
Tel: 01 43 26 67 76

L'Appart

Until midnight, 29 euros can get you the evening's special in this classic restaurant divided into apartment rooms.

9, rue du Colisée, 75008 Paris.
Tel: 01 53 75 42 00

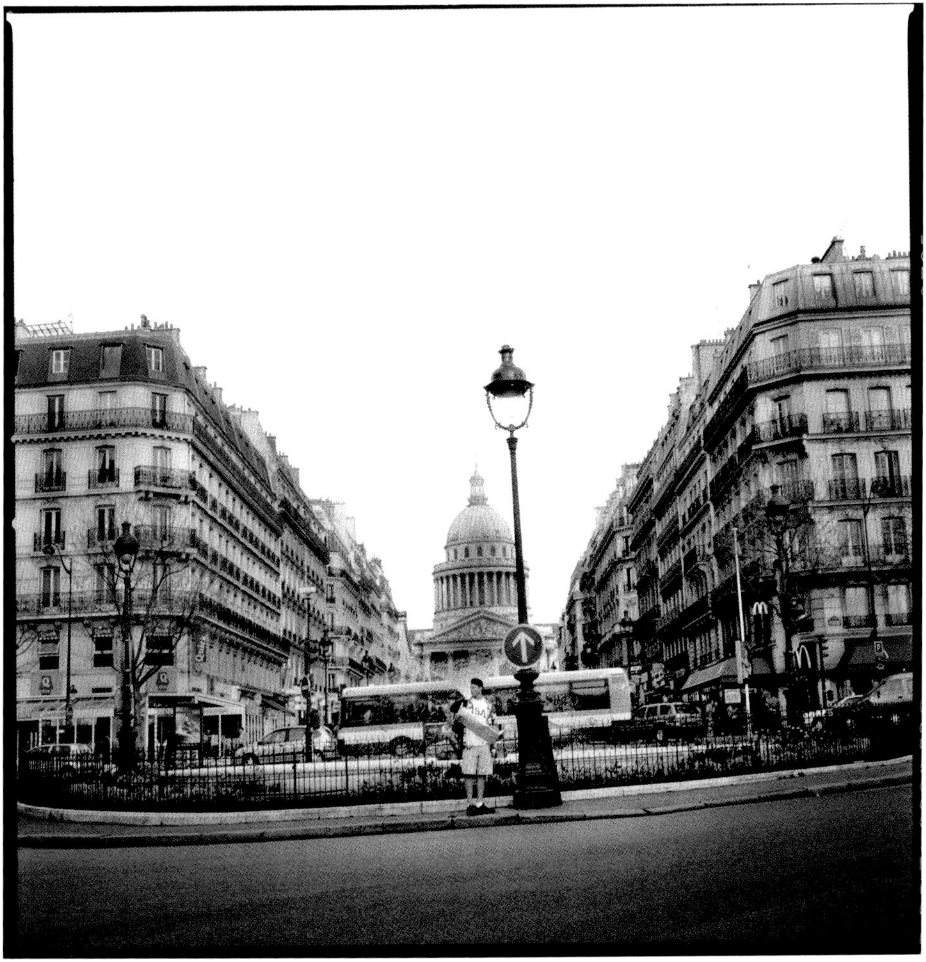

If you miss home cooking, McDonalds is to the right.
(Try the Royal with camembert!)

The best doctor is the cooking pot.

(Savoie)

Open all night

Au Pied de Cochon

Don't miss the onion soup ! 40 euros a la carte.

6, rue de la Coquillière 75001 Paris
Tel: 01 40 13 77 00
www.pieddecochon.com

La Tour de Monthlery

Casual bistro ambiance. 40 euros a la carte.
5, rue des Prouvaires 75001 Paris

Tel: 01 42 36 21 82

L'Alsace

For Sauerkraut until the wee hours.

39 avenue des Champs Elysées 75008 Paris
Tel: 01 53 93 97 00

La Maison de l'Aubrac

Beef, nothing but beef. 30 euros a la carte.

37, rue Marboeuf 75008 Paris
Tel: 01 43 59 05 14

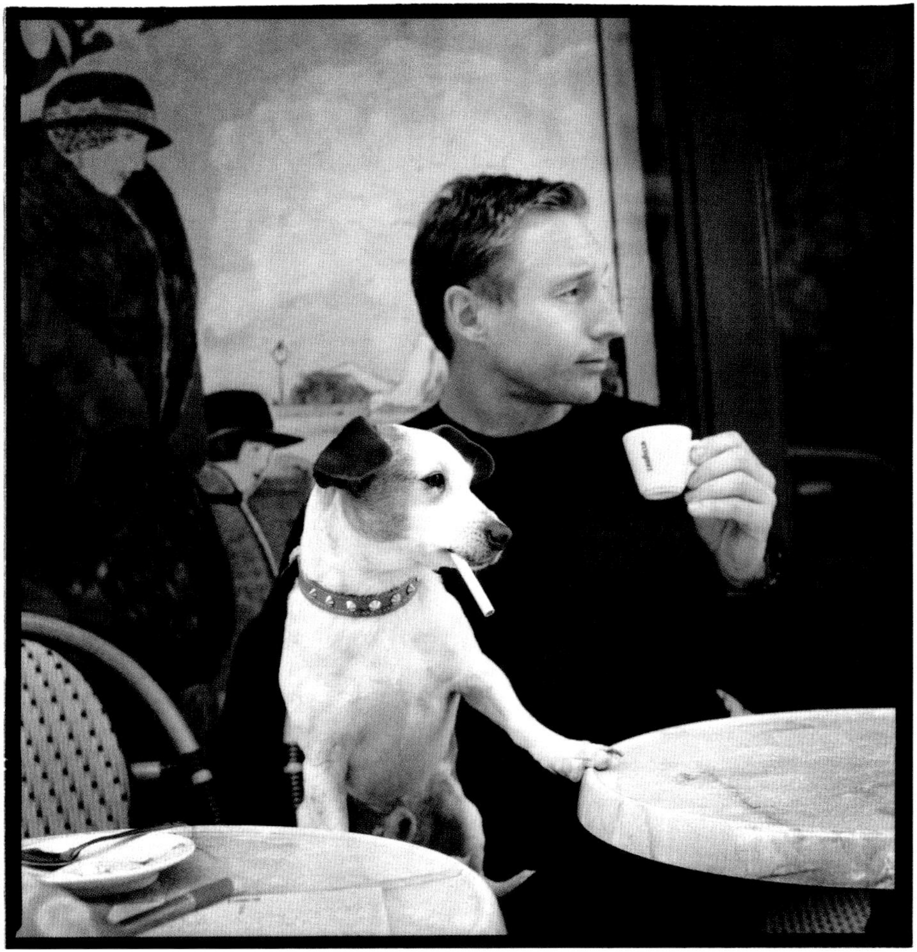

Don't let a Parisian dog smoke you out!!!

Le best chocolate shops.

If you feel guilty, just tell yourself that chocolate is also an aphrodisiac, and less toxic than Viagra.

The best way to overcome temptation is to give in to it.

Fench proverb

La Maison du Chocolat

Every kind of chocolate imaginable, and beverages…

8, bd de la Madeleine 75009 Paris
Tel: 01 47 42 86 52

Christian Constant

The master chocolate-maker, revered by all of Paris. Taste the vervain or jasmine ganache.

37, rue d'Assas 75006 Paris
Tel: 01 53 63 15 15

Debauve & Gallais

This old pharmacy used to sell medicinal chocolate. What a shame it would be to let old habits die.

30, rue des St Pères 75007 Paris
Tel: 01 45 48 54 67, 01 40 39 05 50

A la Petite Fabrique

The entire chocolate selection offered here is made on the premises.

12, rue St Sabin 75011 Paris
Tel: 01 48 05 82 02, 01 43 14 08 82

Cacao et Chocolat

All the pleasures of our childhood are hidden in this shop. Chocolate AND toys!

29, rue de Buci 75006 Paris
Tel: 01 46 33 77 63

parisian delights

The best ice cream

Berthillon

The best and the most famous. Dozens of flavors, from classics to great surprises. Come with patience to spare; the summer waiting lines are long.

31, rue St Louis en L'Isle 75004 Paris
Tel: 01 43 54 31 61

Jadis et Gourmande

Among the city's best ice-cream places. You'll also find delicious chocolates.

39, rue des Archives 75004 Paris
Tel: 01 48 04 08 03

If you mess up a crêpe, you can still make a waffle.

Crepes... how I learned to stop worrying and remember my childhood

La crêpe en l'Isle

13, rue des Deux Ponts 75001 Paris
Tel: 01 43 26 28 68

La crêpe rit du Clown

6, rue des Cannettes 75006 Paris
Tel: 01 46 34 01 02

Créperie St Germain

33, rue St André des Arts 75006 Paris
Tel: 01 43 54 24 41

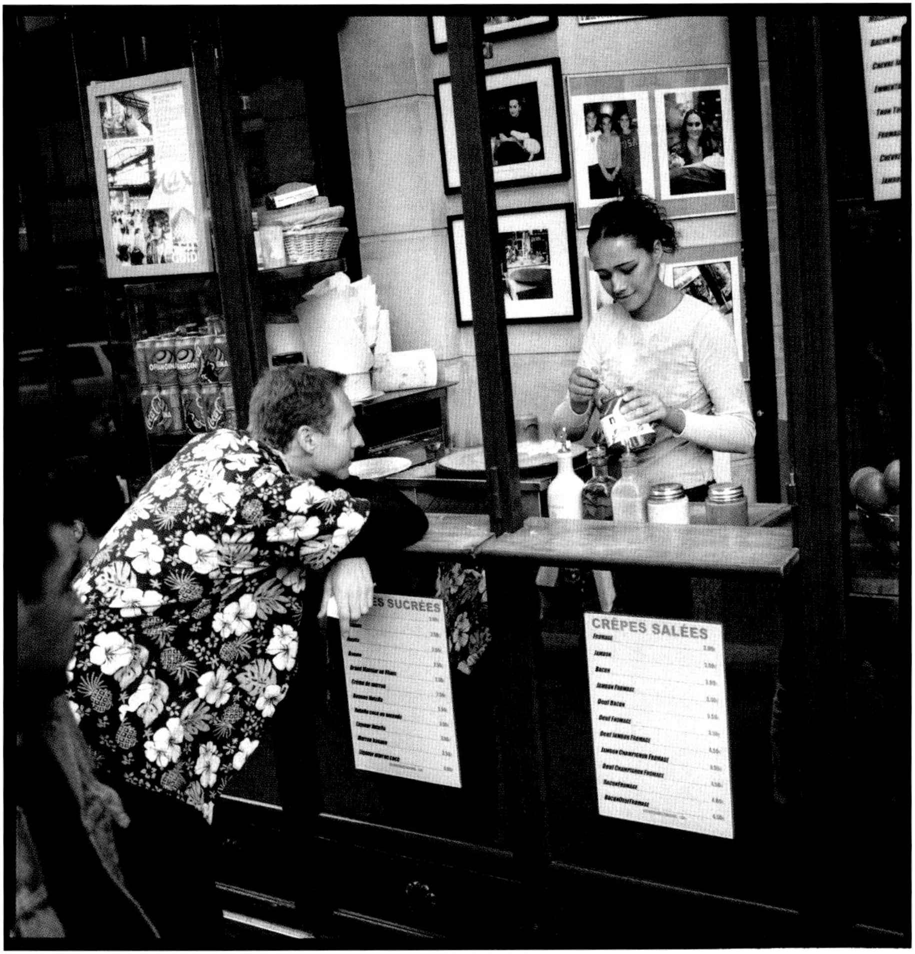

Flattery can get you more chocolate filling in your crêpe, if not pate in your face.

Cellars to drink yourself as silly as a French nobleman

La Dernière Goutte
You can't help drinking it to the last drop.

6, rue de Bourbon le Château 75006 Paris

Tel: 01 43 29 11 62

Les Caves Augé
The oldest cellar in Paris. Marcel Proust was a regular.

116, Bd Haussmann 75008 Paris

Tel: 01 45 22 16 97

Nicolas
This chain of very French wine shops has a retail store in every neighborhood of Paris. Ask for the one closest to you.

132, Bd Raspail 75006 Paris

Tel: 01 43 26 64 36

www.nicolas.com

Two parties are better than a fast.

Fench proverb

Les Caves Taillevent
Half a million bottles await you here. Don't miss the tour of the storerooms.

199, rue du Faubourg St Honoré 75008 Paris

Tel: 01 45 61 14 09

www.taillevent.com

LInconnue de la Bastille
The famous oenologist of Montmarte, Francis Gourdin, transformed the enormous storeroom into a cellar and wine-tasting room. It is evident that he favors the Languedoc Roussillon wines.

12, rue Daval – 12, place de la Bastille 75004 Paris

Tel: 01 47 00 07 80

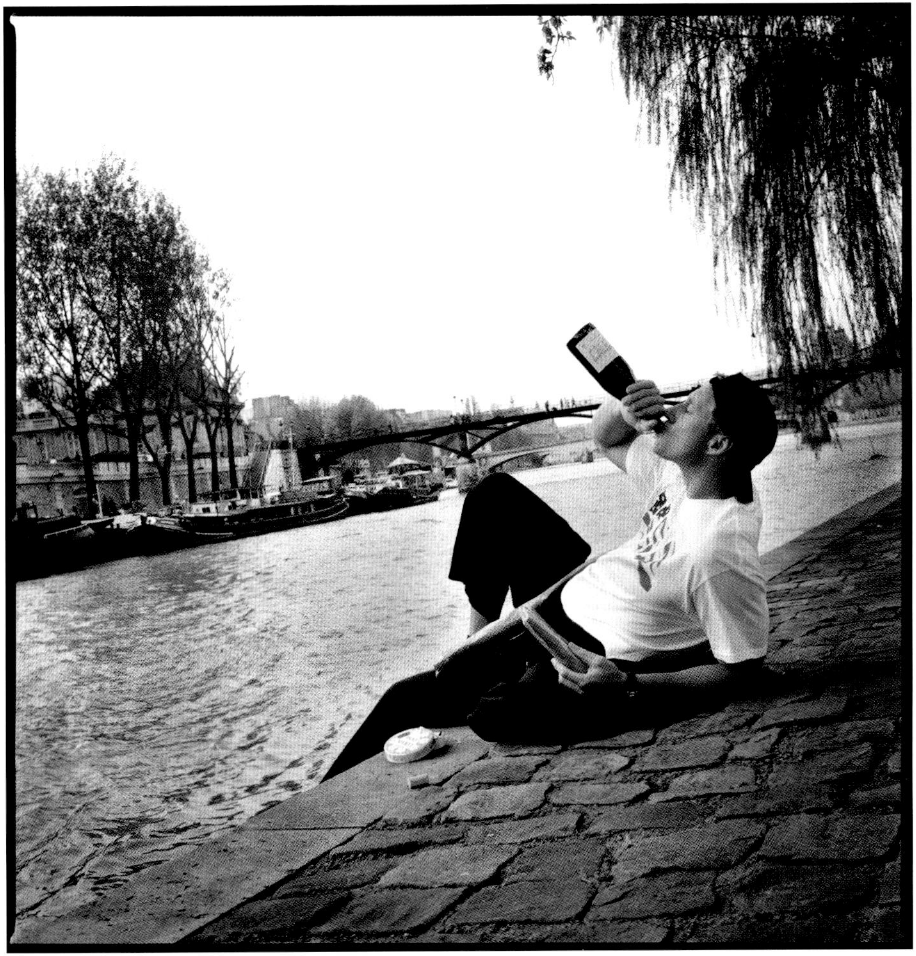

Days of wine and Roses ...
This is the life!

Beauty doesn't put salt in the cooking pot.

The high-end grocery stores - don't be selfish, think of gifts for your friends

Fauchon
So famous that they don't even need a sign.

26, place de la Madeleine 75008 Paris
Tel: 01 47 42 91 10

Hédiard
The direct competitor of the latter, with a bonus of exotic products.

21, place de la Madeleine 75008 Paris
Tel: 01 43 12 88 88
www.hediard.fr

L'Épicerie
Flavored vinegar, quality sauces, jams, honey (try the fig flavored one), and snails… chocolate snails!

51, rue de l'Isle St Louis 75004 Paris
Tel: 01 43 25 20 14

La grande Épicerie de Paris
All the good products are here, opposite the Lutécia hotel.

38, rue de Sèvres 75007 Paris
Tel: 01 44 39 81 00

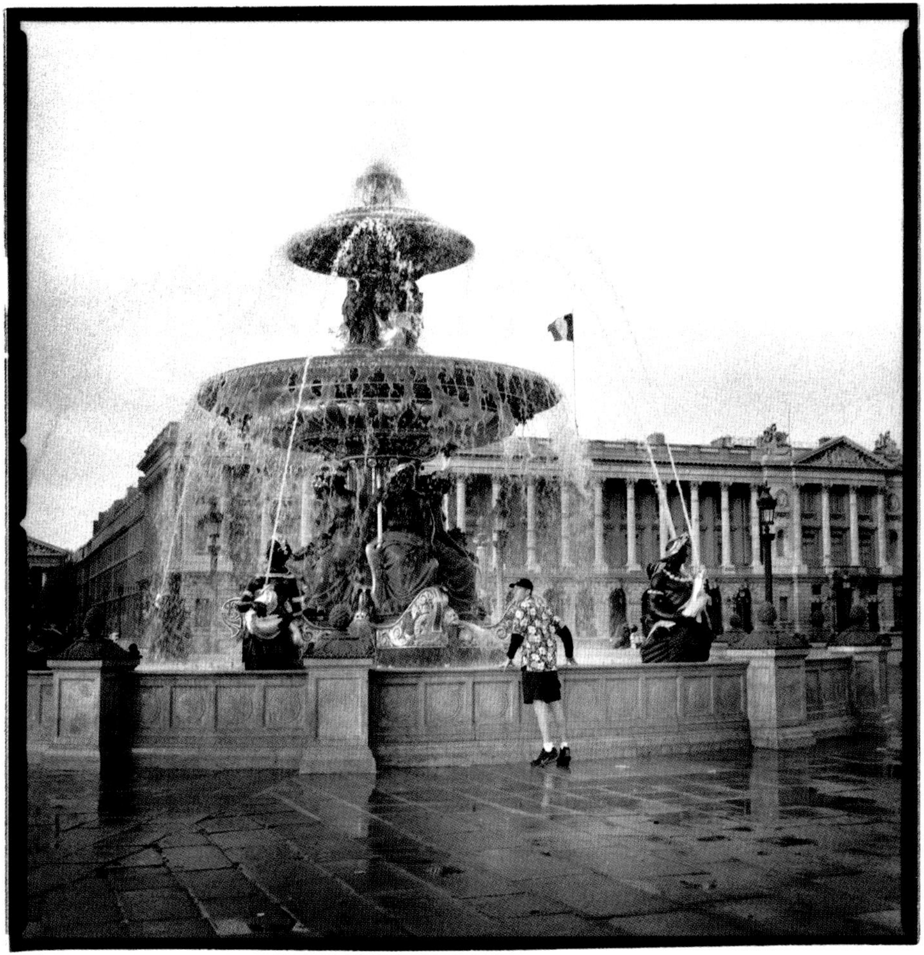

Do tip the fountains.
Don't piss in it.

Better to have a loaf without a cloth, than a cloth without a loaf.

The best baguettes to put in your basket with the liter of red wine

Poujauran

Everything. Everything is excellent here, even the crossed-eyed register lady. A great place for the depressed to fall back into childhood and cry warm tears.

20, rue Jean Nicot 75007 Paris
Tel: 01 43 17 35 20

Paul

You'll be trapped in this haven for good bread and authentic pastry.

77, rue de Seine 75006 Paris
Tel: 01 55 42 02 23

Boulangeries Julien

Voted the city's best baguette several times. We thought it might be a sign.

75, rue St Honoré 75001 Paris
Tel: 01 42 36 24 83

Poîlane

One kind of bread – dark and tender with a thick floury crust. A taste never matched. Rumor has it they use to finance right-winged extremist Jean-Marie Le Pen, a rumor most certainly started by jealous competitors. C'est la vie.

8, rue du Cherche Midi 75006 Paris
Tel: 01 45 48 42 59

49, Bd de Grenelle 75015 Paris
Tel: 01 45 79 11 49

www.poilane.fr

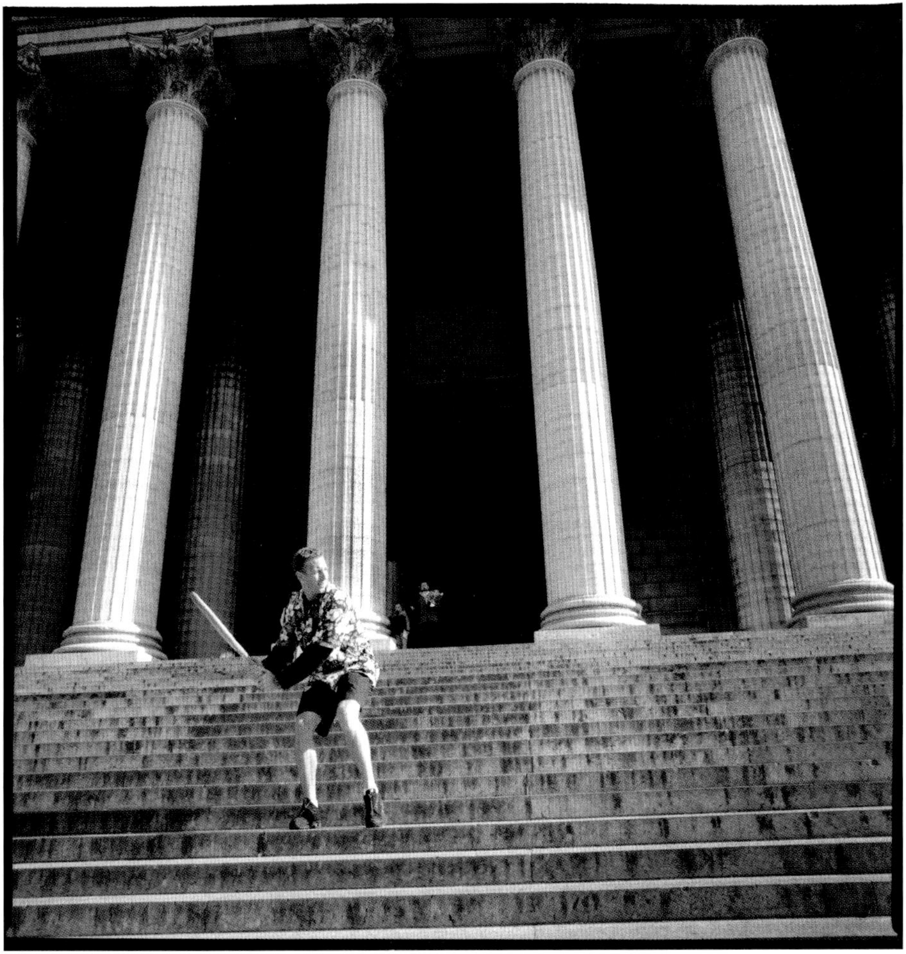

Golf the Parisian way...
with baguettes and fromage de chêvre!!!

Au Pain Bien Cuit

To have it just like Chirac. Yes sir. Chirac likes it well done, so René does it well.

111, Bd Haussemann 75008 Paris
Tel: 01 42 65 06 25

The pastry that will make your scale scream for heavenly mercy

Pierre Hermé

The cakes here are expensive because they are like jewels. The Isphahan and the chocolate-passion fruit macaroons are to-die-for. The Isphahan and the chocolate-passion fruit macaroons are an absolute must.

72, rue Bonaparte 75006 Paris
Tel: 01 43 54 47 77

185 rue Vaugirard 75015 Paris
01 47 83 29 72

Two parties are better than a fast.
Fench proverb

Christian Constant

If you don't like to walk, wait in line, keep quiet and look profoundly inspired for eight hours, then the immaculate chocolate collection of this pastry chef will advantageously replace a Sunday visit to the Louvre museum.

37, rue d'Assas 75006 Paris
Tel: 01 53 63 15 15

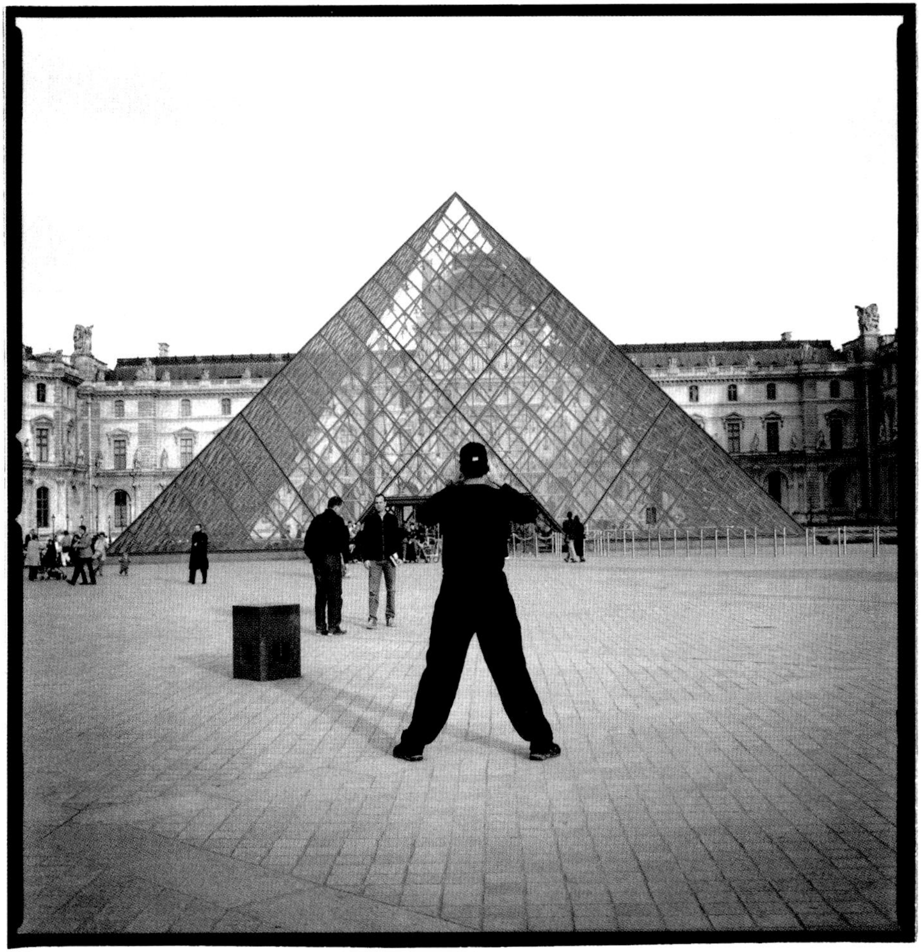

Doesn't this belong to Egypt ?

Everyone knows how to be good...after the fact.

French proverb

Bon
With a name meaning "good" need we say more? Try the classics – lemon tarts, éclairs, cream puffs, flans...

159 rue St Jacques 75005 Paris
Tel: 01 43 54 26 44

Strohrer
Regional specialties. Because they don't just eat sauerkraut in Alsace.

51, rue de Montorgueil 75002 Paris
Tel: 01 42 33 38 20

Toraya
Surprising and refined. Adventure into the world of Japanese pastry, where you will have it with both butter and cream.

10, rue St Florentin 75001 Paris
Tel: 01 42 60 13 00
www.toraya.group.co.jp/paris/

La Bague de Kenza
If you can't get your hands on a French lover, make up for it with the cakes of Arabian nights. Honey, chopped almonds, and sugar in every way possible complete these North African specialties.

106, rue St Maur 75011 Paris
Tel: 01 43 14 93 15

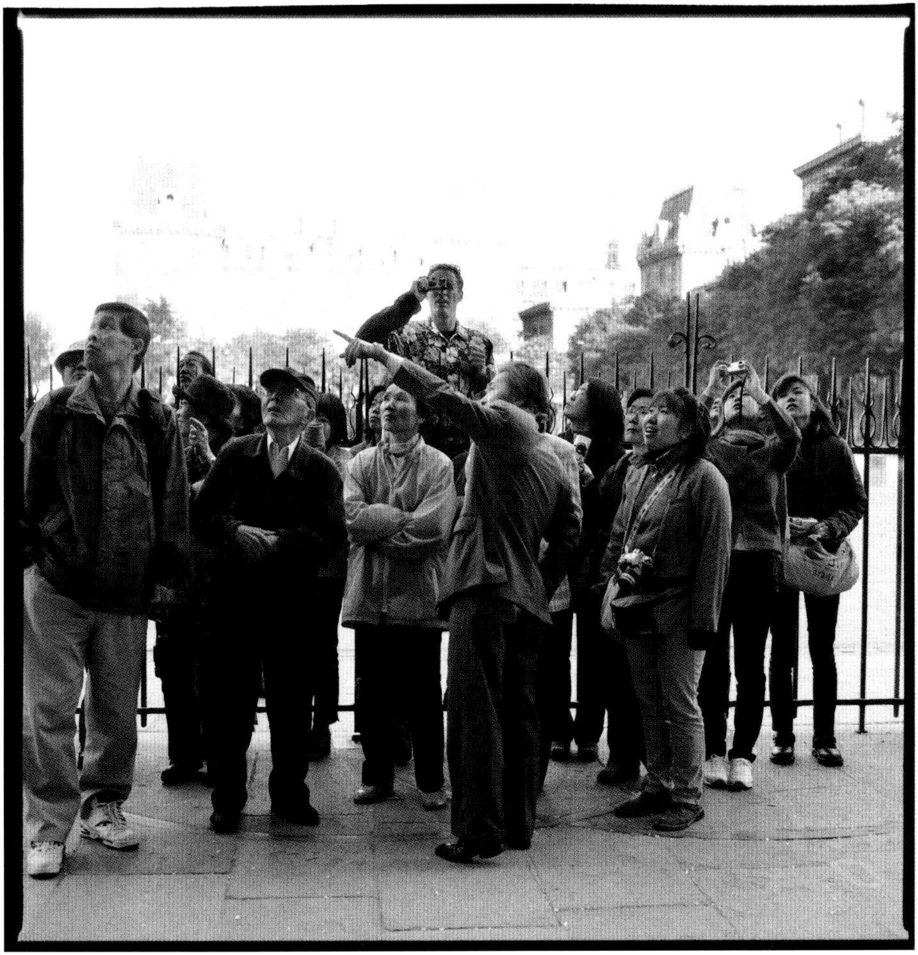

Pay attention to the guide or you'll
miss the point.

It's better to fart with friends than die alone.

French proverb from Auvergne

The smelliest cheese in town

Barthélémy

51, rue de Grenelle 75007 Paris
Tel: 01 42 22 82 24

Quatrehomme

62, rue de Sèvres 75007 Paris
Tel: 01 47 34 33 45

Firmin

79 rue de Courcelles 75017 Paris
Tel: 01 43 80 36 42

Fromagerie Montmarte

9 rue du Ponteau 75007 Paris
Tel: 01 46 06 26 03

Alain Dubois

80, rue de Tocqueville 75017 Paris
Tel: 01 42 27 11 38

79, rue de Courcelles 75017 Paris
Tel: 01 43 80 36 42

Chez Virginie

54, rue Damrémont 75018 Paris
Tel: 01 46 06 76 54

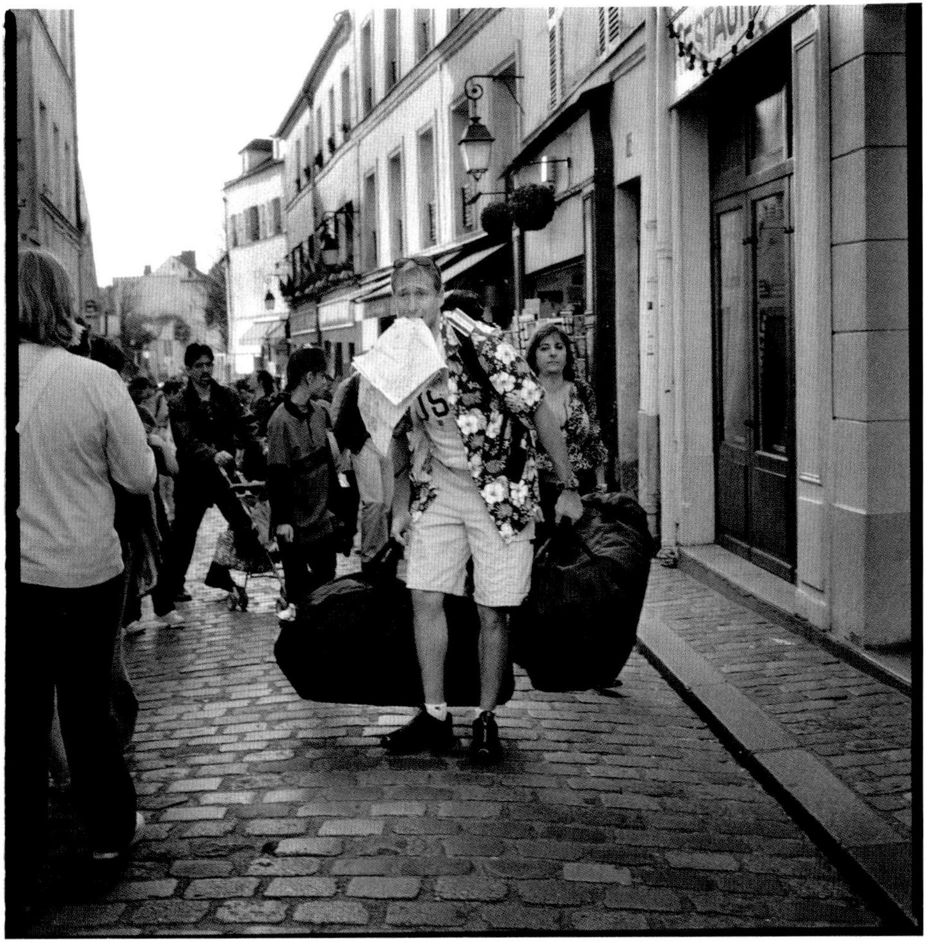

The metro is fun, but if you want to look like you know where your going, Take a cab.

Spending the night in Paris

Hotels for the eye and the mind

You just have to be where the pot boils.

Hôtel Istria: A crash course in Art History for Dummies. You'll certainly appreciate an establishment where you can study your Art History and crack up at the same time. The greatest and most financially broke have spent nights under this roof – Francis Picabia, Rainier Maria Rilke … Aragon. Just ask a few questions at the front desk to learn some naughty and scandalous stories about other big names that have made a mark in French Art History here. Rooms run from 92 to 100 euros.

29 rue Campagne Première 75014 Paris
Tel : 01 43 20 91 82
hotel.istria@wanadoo.fr

Timhôtel: Studying Art history for those who like to show off. If you like studying your Art History with the conviction of your undeniable intelligence, this is the establishment for you. Each of the five floors is dedicated to an artist: Lautrec, Utrillo, Picasso, Matisse, Renoir. The more you go up, the more you savor. Rooms 417 and 517 offer an amazing view of all of Paris. Celebrate your newly attained culture with champagne. At 30 euros a cocktail, avoid snooty intellectual grimacing. Rooms for 125 euros.

11, rue Ravignan (Place Emile Goudeau) 75018 Paris
Tel : 01 42 55 74 79
www.timhotel.com

Nouvel Hôtel: Color-Blind Special
The unique decorative styles by Laura Ashley ensures that each room is a different color. Rooms run from 104 to 128 euros.

24, avenue Bel Air 75012 Paris
Tel : 01 43 43 01 81
www.nouvel-hotel-paris.com

best hotels

One must never say: « Fountain, I shall nor drink your water » All you need is a swim in great waters.

The best hotel rooms for taking a bath

Ile St Louis district Hôtel St Paul Le Marais: Ask for the rooms with a jacuzzi. Near the Vosges Square, in the heart of the Marais, this ancient stone building will please all the lovers of true and rustic ambiances. The furniture is simple yet stylish and modern. ... Room 27 recommended.

8, rue de Sévigné 75004 Paris
Tel : 01 48 04 97 27
Fax : 01 48 87 37 04
Price : from 150 euros to 190 euros for the rooms with a jacuzzi.
www.hotelsaintpaullemarais.com

Hôtel Brighton: Take a bath while admiring the Tuileries Gardens. Built during the height of Rue de Rivoli's glory, the rooms of this hotel are absolutely charming. The large windows open up to a balcony from which you can admire the Tuileries Gardens or the hotel's courtyards. Ask for the renovated rooms if you want a large bathroom. Room 70 recommended.

218 rue de Rivoli 75001 Paris
Tel : 01 47 03 61 61
Fax : 01 42 60 41 78
www.benecom.com/france/paris/brighton/

Hôtel de Nesle: For a Turkish bath in your room. Ask for room 4 on the second floor, where you can relax and loose yourself to a Saharan universe with primitive motifs straight out of the Tibesti frescos. The Turkish bath opens up into a small courtyard and the arabesque ceramics will charm you with its exotica. A true paradise of sensuality for only 75 euros per night.

7, rue de Nesle 75006 Paris
Tel : 01 43 54 62 41

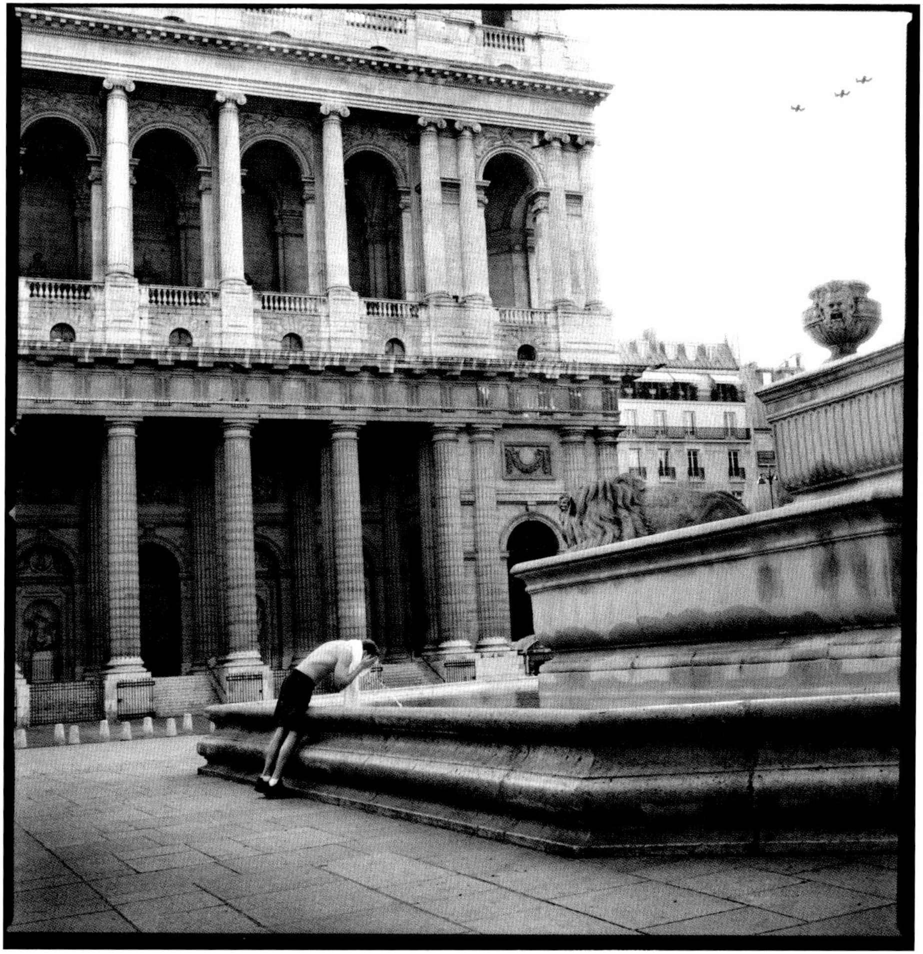

Don't bathe in the fountains ...
unless you want a room with bars!

Hotel des St Pères: Taking a bath in a 17th Century palace. This establishment is the former mansion of Daniel Gittard, a 17th Century architect who was also the favorite of Louis XIV. The rooms are all charming, and run from 147 euros (for a view of the courtyard) to 215 euros (for a view of the Tuileries Gardens). Room 100… 17th Century … Versailles. This beautiful surface rises to a 30-foot ceiling and has a bathroom finished with tinted windows and an oval tub, separated only by a folding screen. The giant loft-room has a mezzanine bathroom…. well worth it!

65, rue des St Pères 75006 Paris
Tel : 01 45 44 50 00
Fax : 01 45 44 90 83

Hôtel des Croisés: For the bonus chimney
All charming Art Nouveau. Ask for a large bathroom, you'll get an immeasurable one with a chimney to boot. Each room has its own history. So, get moving and ask for tales. Rooms from 77 to 118 euros.

63, rue St Lazare 75009 Paris
Tel : 01 48 74 78 24
www.charmingsmallhotels.com

Only the lid really knows what's in the cooking pot

(Guadeloupe)

The best hotel rooms for lovemaking

Hotel Opera Maintenon: For the hard-to-please who need to take center stage. What? It doesn't excite you to yourself in the mirror? Complete with innumerable indecent mirrors that cover the walls of the 17th Century décor, this place will rock you into the deepest oblivion of passion and desire, plunging you into a naughty mood and into the hidden morals that have gorged these rooms in the Great Century... If walls could talk! The floral wallpapered alcoves await the tender flirt of first time couples. As for miscellaneous paraphernalia to go with the room, consult other sections of this book. Rooms from 75 to 90 euros.

36 rue Sainte Anne 75001 Paris
Tel : 01 42 97 41 53
www.hotel-opera-maintenon.com, opera.maintenon@proximedia.fr

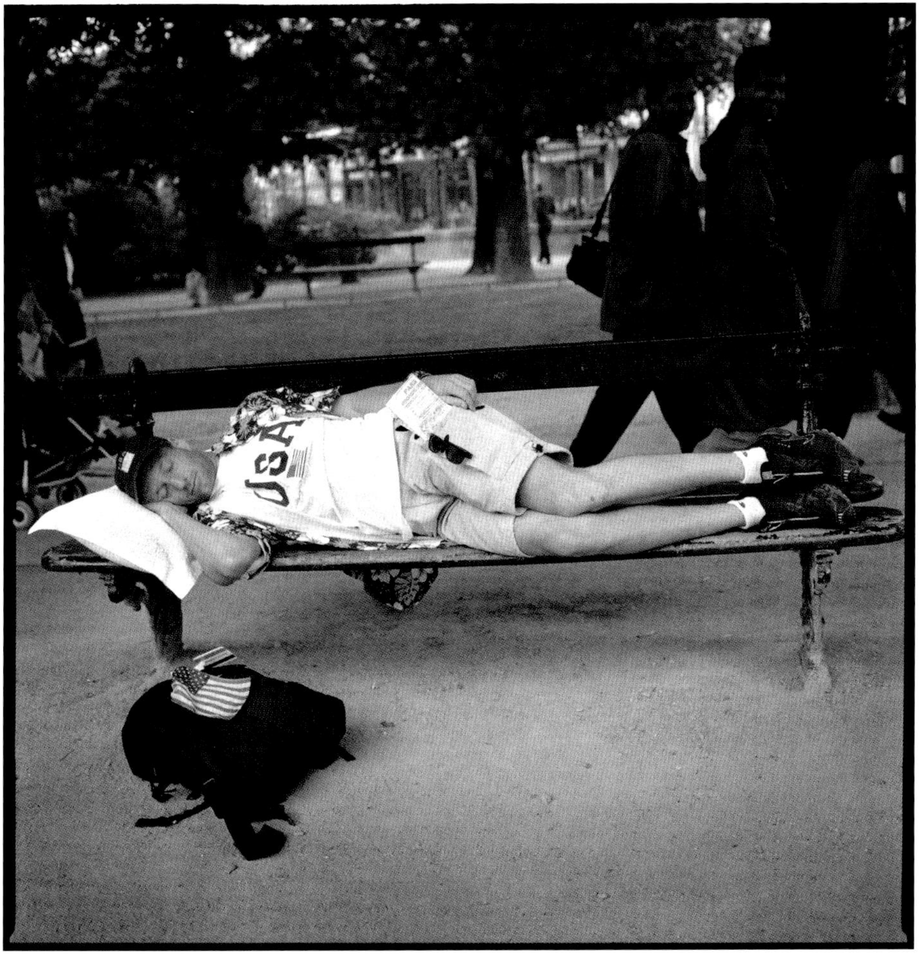

Keep an open eye on your baggage!

Between soups and love affairs, soups win every time.

Hôtel Rotary: Brush up on your Kama Sutra love techniques…for cheap. In order to fully explore the cultural intricacies of the sex game, you'd have to stay in all of the rooms in this establishment. The selection of themes will keep you intrigued and coming back for more – the Baroque mosaic room with its verdigris statue, the Chinese room with the jade bed reflecting in the ceiling mirror, the pink boudoir room with soft light and Art Deco furniture, and the list goes on… Inviting a casual lover there is a great idea. As for couples, everything's open for negotiation. With rooms from 40 to 60 euros, you'll get a big bang for your buck.

4, rue de Vintimille 75009 Paris
Tel : 01 48 74 26 39
www.hotel.rotary@wanadoo.fr

Hôtel Acacias Etoile: A very charming hotel. Rooms are very cosy. Newly redecorated rooms. Offers great breakfast and bar.

11, rue des Acacias 75016 Paris
Tel: 01 43 80 60 22
Fax: 01 48 88 96 40
www.hotel-acacias.etoile.com

L'Hôtel: Brush up on your Kama Sutra love techniques…if you can spare the change.
Every room here also has a distinct theme – the Pagoda room with sculpted bamboo, the African room with leopard and other exotic patterns, the Viollet-le-Duc with Gothic features… All revisited by the great Jacques Garcia. You can also swing with lovers between here and the Hotel Rotary. Advice: leave jealousy at home. Rooms from 295 to 595 euros.

13, rue des Beaux Arts 75006 Paris
Tel : 01 44 41 99 00
www.l-hotel.com, reservation@l-hotel.com

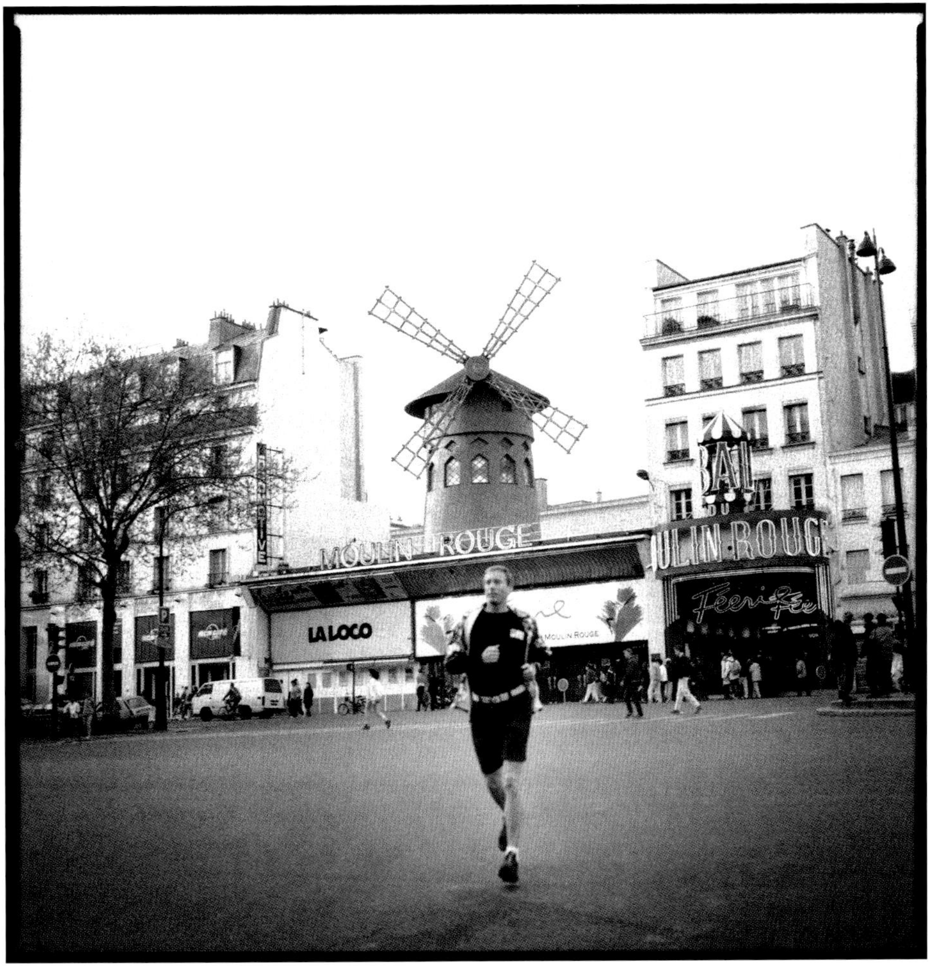

Oh ... I think I am in love !!!

The knife shall never appease heresy.

French adage

Villa Caroline: Do it Emmanuelle style

Dim lighting and crimson velvet will hypnotize you and your partner into your most erotic alter egos, unleashing a delicious sensation of the forbidden for you to explore. Ask for the rattan room to relive scenes of famous erotic films. Or go for the room with the circular bed that rests at the top of the last staircase. Your parents were right – nothing like the classics!

85, rue de la Pompe 75016 Paris
Tel : 01 45 04 05 20
www.leshotelsdeparis.com

Going from the bed to the bath and from the bath to the bed, without separating or burning yourselves; have you tried

Villa Royale: The naughty bath.

In the heart of Pigalle, it's a guaranteed change of scenery. You couldn't find anything more old-fashioned – gold, fake rubies, ostentatiously colored ornaments, violet taffetas, crazy lighting, lamenting Arabic music. The rooms are baptized with names of French stars – Deneuve, Bardot, St. Laurent. Try the room with a hot tub and the burning gas fire. If this doesn't get you off, try harder. Rooms from 230 to 270 euros.

2, rue Duperré 75009 Paris
Tel : 01 55 31 78 78

royale@leshotelsdeparis.com

For the lazy ones: the best views from the bed

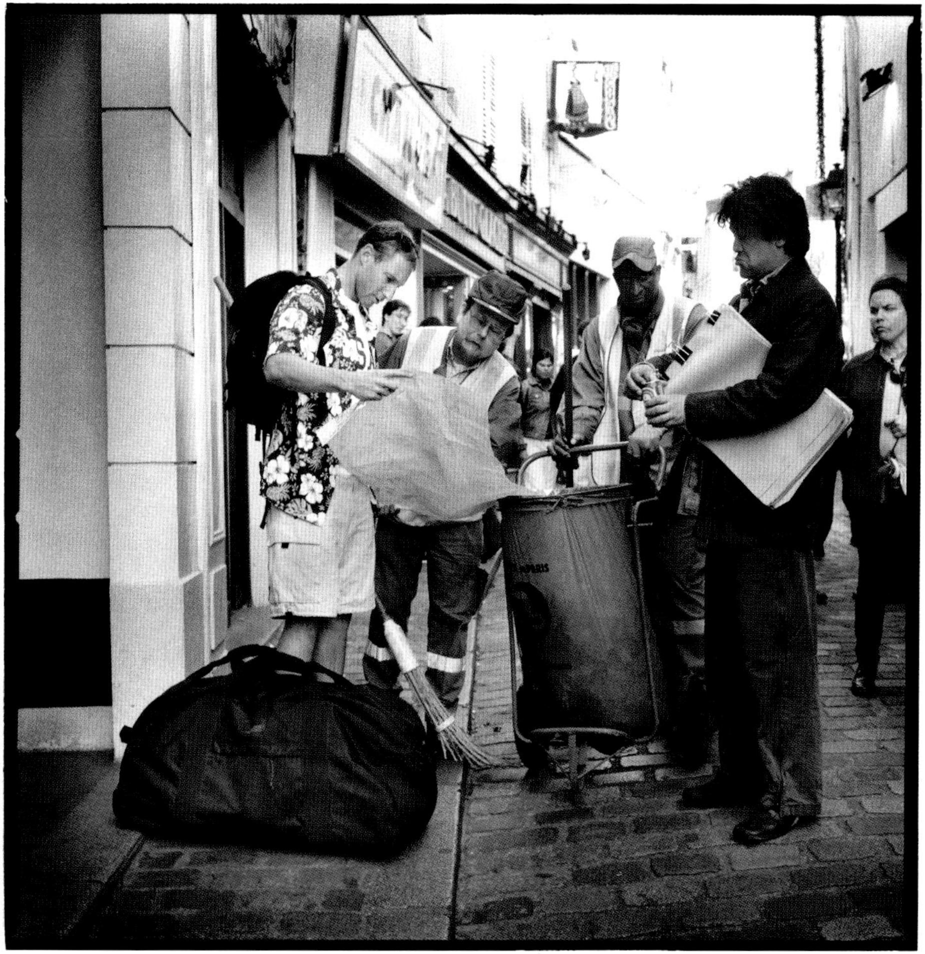

Don't even think of asking directions
if you don't speak French!

Often the petticoats mock the pants

Hôtel du Quai Voltaire: For playing the artist, tormented by their creative vertigo. Room 52 of this 18th Century abbey, between the Pont du Carrousel and the Pont Royal, offers a spectacular view of the Seine, its bridges and the Louvre. Room 32 is where Pissaro painted his famous Pont Royal in 1903. Oscar Wilde might have been a backward snob declaring he would not spend time looking out a window, but other greats such as Hemingway, Sibellius and Wagner have spent their nights here devouring the Parisian lights to feast their eyes. For masochists, do as Baudelaire did and take the room that's lost at the end of the dark hallway, the one that opens out to the rear of the building. This room has a tired couch and a low, back-breaking desk lit only by a small window. In this room, Baudelaire would whip his mistress between the composition of two verses. You too can use this room to satisfy your fetishes. Rooms from 122 euros.

19, Quai Voltaire 75007 Paris
Tel : 01 42 61 50 91
www.quaivoltaire.fr

Sofitel Paris Bercy: Calling all exhibitionists
On the 9th floor of this new luxury establishment, you can experience a glass duplex that can open three of its four walls. Relax on the sycamore furniture and simply enjoy the beauty of this fantastic capital. The National Library, the Seine, the Notre Dame and the Pantheon will all be there, at your feet. This erotic setting is perfect for the purest and sexiest adventures imaginable. At your crucial moment with your head upside down in love, don't be surprised to find voyeur government officials in the next building taking notes. A guaranteed sensation for all parties. For practice, start with the enormous burgundy curtains drawn. Rooms from 220 to 500 euros. For an orgasm that big, you gotta pay the price.

1, avenue des terroirs Français 75012 Paris
Tel : 01 44 67 34 00
www.sofitel.com

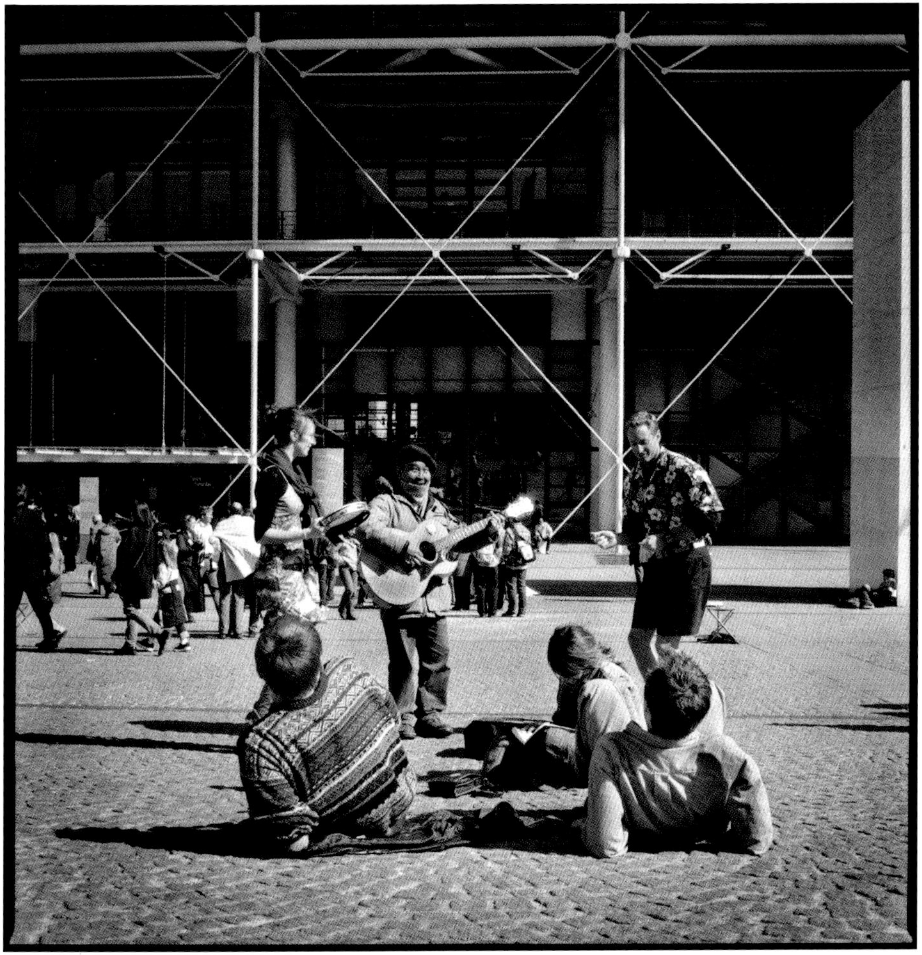

Dance in the Streets, keep in rhythm
but don't quit your day job.

Chances are that when you're well dressed, you won't happen upon your mother-in-law.

Proverb from Guadeloupe

Timhôtel Italie: So as So that your stories stay original from those of other Americans returning from Paris.

Behind its plain appearance and a décor without history, this hotel has a hidden jewel – the rooms on the top floor. From there you can admire Little Russia and Little Alsace. So what? That's exactly what your neighbors will ask, assuming that all you need to know is the Champs Elysees, the Notre Dame and St. Germain des Pres. Not so. Here, you'll find the highlights of la Butte aux Cailles, a small Parisian village that you shouldn't miss. With its quaint houses, roses and wisteria lining the winding streets, it's a cozy village not yet invaded by the dramatic crowd of Montmarte. Rooms for 90 euros.

22, rue Barrault 75013 Paris
Tel : 01 45 80 67 67
www.my-paris-hotel.com

Hôtel Parc St Séverin: For true lies.

If you want your posse to believe that you went to St. Tropez with Johnny Hallyday and Laetitia Casta, stay in room 7 where you can tan naked on the 90 square foot terrace with a 180 degree view of Paris. If you want to reconstruct the ambiance of the Var's nocturnal capital, go in groups of 10 (it comes out to 26 euros per person). Choose from your choice of companions among the young, the beautiful, the cool, the crazy, the superficial or the alcoholics. Makes your adventure more exciting to tell than the real story.

22, rue de la Parcheminerie 75005 Paris
Tel : 01 43 54 32 17
www.esprit-de-france.com

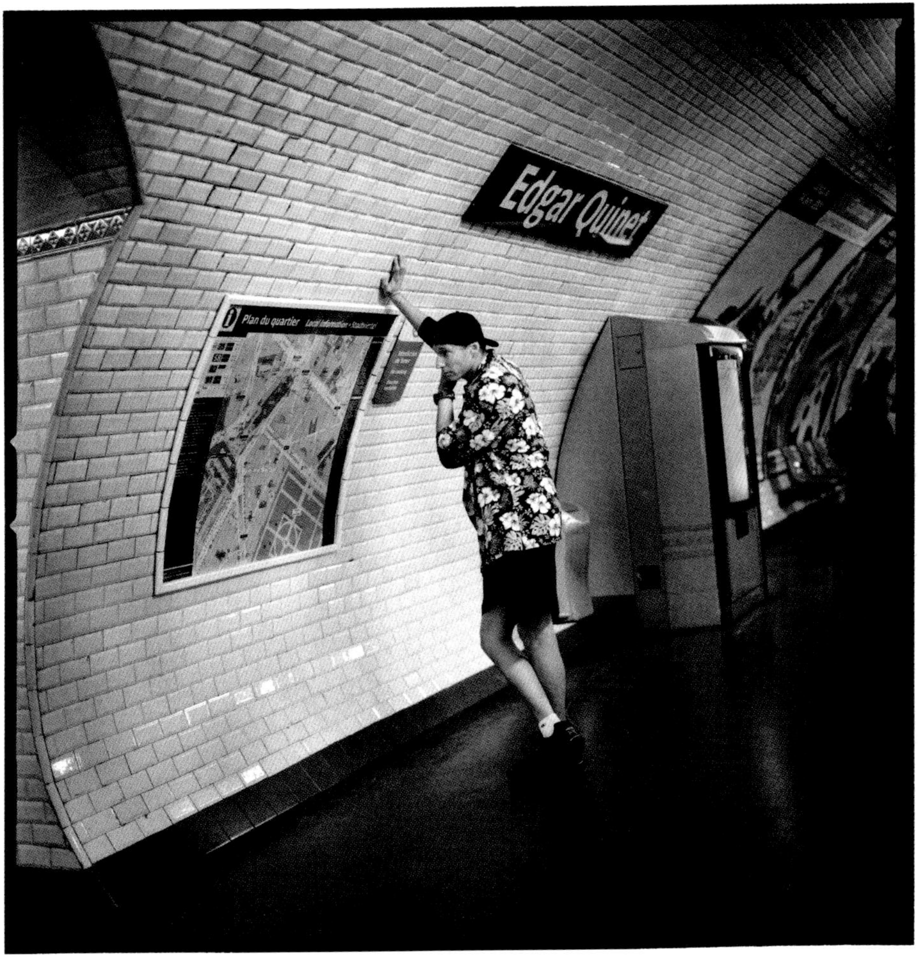

Wish I'd brought my hand-held GPS...

the best Spas

Nuxe

The first spa by the famous brand Nuxe has just opened its doors to everyone's delight. You'll discover the shape and firmness treatment, which uses the new line of Amazonian-plant-based products from Spa Tonific in conjunction with massages, firmness creams, reflexology, body shaping and powdering. 140 euros per treatment (1 1/4 hours).

32 rue de Montorgueil, 75002 Paris
Tel : 01 55 80 71 40

www.nuxe.com

Villains drink water.

Fench proverb

Spa Les 5 Mondes

A jewel of an institute hidden in an unsuspected square of the Opéra district. Blissfully serene, this Eastern-inspired spa offers Japanese ritual massages as well as Ayurvedic, Taoist, Indonesian, Maghrebin treatments. Modern designs are finished in tones of orange and blue, and a very inviting use of chromatherapy on mood. You can even choose the color of your sauna from blue, pink or yellow. Another exceptional feature, which is unique in Paris, is a Japanese cedar bathtub. Japanese baths are 45 euros, the Rituel Majeur Corps Esprit treatment and its seven appointments are 380 euros.

6, square de L'Opéra-Louis-Jouvet, 75009 Paris
Tel : 01 42 66 00 60
www.cinqmondes.com

Les Bains du Marais

The most elegant spa n Paris. For those special days, go all the way! Complete with saunas, manicures, pedicures, facials, shampoos and hair-styling for 200 euros.

31-33 rue des Blancs Manteaux, 75004 Paris
Tel : 01 44 61 02 02
www.lesbainsdumarais.com

health & beauty

You can't stay very long in a perfume shop without leaving with the smell.

Fench proverb

(Méry)

Women's special: **Anne Semonin**

Do like Juliette Binoche and Isabelle Adjani, visit Anne Sémonin's spa when in Paris. This luxurious, white-tiled day spa with honey colored beauty studios, an annex to the elegant Hotel le Bristol, is an oasis of serenity in the heart of Paris's bustling Right Bank shopping district. The treatments are custom made to meet the needs of your skin type, age and taste. Ask for Sémonin's facial-and-pedicure, a double-whammy treatment involving a simultaneous facial and luxurious three-part pedicure: an in-depth nail session, followed by a fabulous calf-and-foot massage and a high-gloss buffing (140 euros). Try the skin preparations using white seaweed, salt from the Dead Sea, lavender, lemon and corn germ oils. Reduce tired bags, wrinkles and redness with an eye serum treatment (60 euros). Also great is the anti-jetlag treatment with its invigorating volcanic mud. There's a different tea available each day. As for massages – any type you can imagine, with a background of ocean or river soundtracks to perfect the mood. A must do – get the shiatsu in a tent of minimal décor with a fireplace, a futon and a tatami. You'll breath in the pure air of the mountains thanks to a machine sent from heaven. Discover the secrets of the goddesses!

108 Rue du Faubourg St. Honoré
Paris 75008
01 331 42 66 24 22

Men's special: **Institut Nickel, Printemps Haussemann**

While your beloved revels in the height of ecstasy at Anne Semonin's, go get your own hot bod brushed up on the banks the Seine. Here you can get waxed in any way you wish – swimmer's back, cyclist legs, boxer's chest, love handles, double chin… How about just-for-fun or after-party massage with special de-hangover agents.

64 Bd Haussemann 75009 Paris
Tel : 01 42 82 64 75
www.nickel.fr

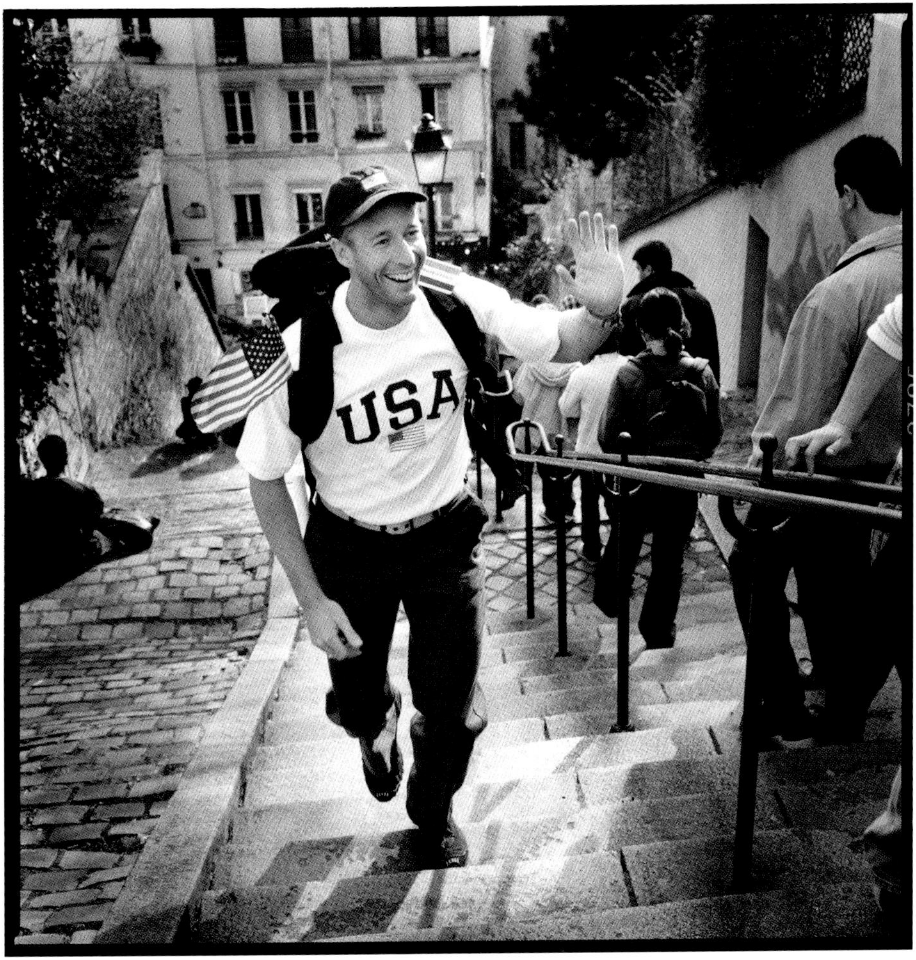

this is not a beauty pageant ...
you don't have to say hello to everyone.

You'll find your fancy under the filth.

Fench proverb, from Nantes

For couples: dare to try the **Thermes du Royal Monceau**
The Parisian palace on avenue Hoche houses 1400 square meters of fitness center around the hotel's garden, including a pool, sauna, and balneotherapy. Treat yourself to a relaxation cure, a la carte (90 euros per relaxation day, 170 euros per beauty treatment day).

39, avenue Hoche 75008 Paris
Tel : 01 42 99 85 66
www.royalmonceau.com

the must sees

Le Nails Bar du Bon Marché

To give your nails the best care, look no further – the Shu Uemura treatment hydrates and brightens nails, including a Japanese bath with Yuzu lemon, humidification with Rosemary Deep Sea Water and an application of a lemon extract based mask. 38 euros for your nails au naturel. 45 euros for the personalized French manicure. From June to August.

24, rue de Sevres 75007 Paris
Tel : 01 42 22 33 49

Salons du Palais Royal Shiseido

The famous perfume creator, Serge Lutens, serves as an invisible master of ceremonies in this diabolical boudoir. Violet décor with an Arabic feel combines the extremes of rough and refined. Vials filled with maddening juices of aromas discernable only with your noses in the bottles. Musc … et Lavande. Lose your senses in this labyrinth of scents. Here, you'll learn once more that selling yourself to the devil is expensive.

142, Galerie de Valois, 75001 Paris in the Palais Royal gardens.
Tel : 01 49 27 09 09
www.salons-shiseido.com

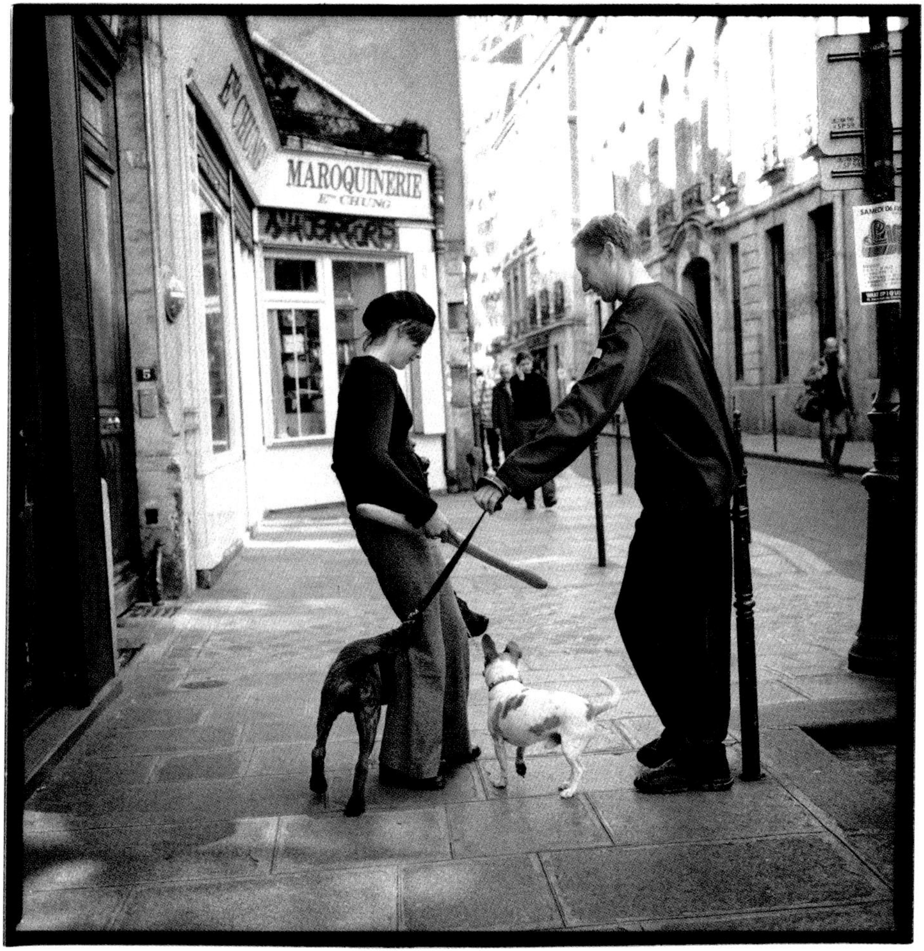

Even dogs fall in love in Paris

A healthy body is the most valuable possession.

Fench proverb

La Sultane de Sabah

You'll want to clean out this shop of a thousand pleasures. that you'll find yourself engulfed by consuming sensuality. Jasmine, rose, amber, musk, orange flower and other botanical fragrances will drive you mad with pleasure. There's a salon hidden behind the backdoor, which you shouldn't hesitate to open even if you have only an hour to spare. Drop your man off at Le Roi de Salomon, the male version of this miraculous paradise two buildings down the street.

8, bis rue Bachaumont 75002 Paris
01 40 41 90 95
www.iwebu.com/french/_directory/_shopping/shopping_01.html

Colette

Needless to introduce this fashion institution, so trendy, trendy. With the unmistakable address of the rue St. Honore, the beauty products displayed here may be minimalist but they are sure to be the season's best brands – Nars, bumble and Bumble, Kiels, Joelle Ciocco, etc.

213, rue St.Honoré
Tel: 01 55 35 33 90
www.colette.fr

Caron

Founded in 1904, Caron has become a luxurious theatre of scents. Go there dreaming about the great decadent era of loose morals as you stroll your nose through the masterpieces of refinement – Narcisse Noir, Narcisse Blanc, Fleur de Rocaille, French Cancan, Rose, etc.

34, avenue Montaigne 75008 Paris
Tel : 01 47 23 40 82

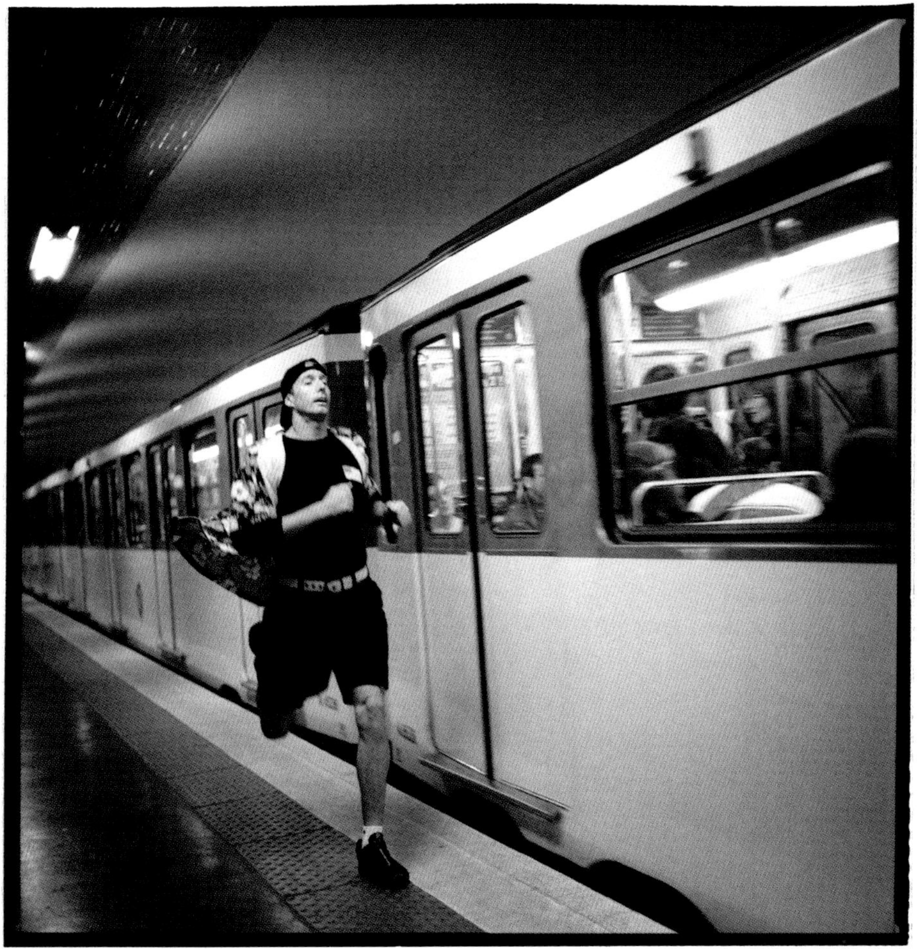

Don't sweat it, the métro come every 2 minutes!

Fine hair will be clever.

Fench proverb,

from Orléans

Diptyque

Founded in 1961, this perfumery will take you on a journey across the ages, drifting through the scents of the world and almost makes you regret being in Paris. The box office hit here is L'Ombre dans L'Eau.

34, Bd St Germain 75005 Paris
Tel : 01 43 26 45 27
www.diptyqueparis.com

Muji

No perfumes here but essentials galore. This "no brand" shop offers quality Japan concentrate at very reasonable prices. In a minimalist setting, you'll find a variety of goodies such as beauty basics, instruments and utensils of all sorts, lingerie and clothes, dishes, paper products and even interior decoration. A must see.

27 rue St. Sulpice 75006 Paris
01 46 34 01 10

30 rue St. Sulpice 75006
01 44 07 37 30

18 pass Reales 75001 Paris
01 44 88 56 56

47 rue Francs Bourgeois 75004 Paris
01 49 96 41 41
www.muji.fr

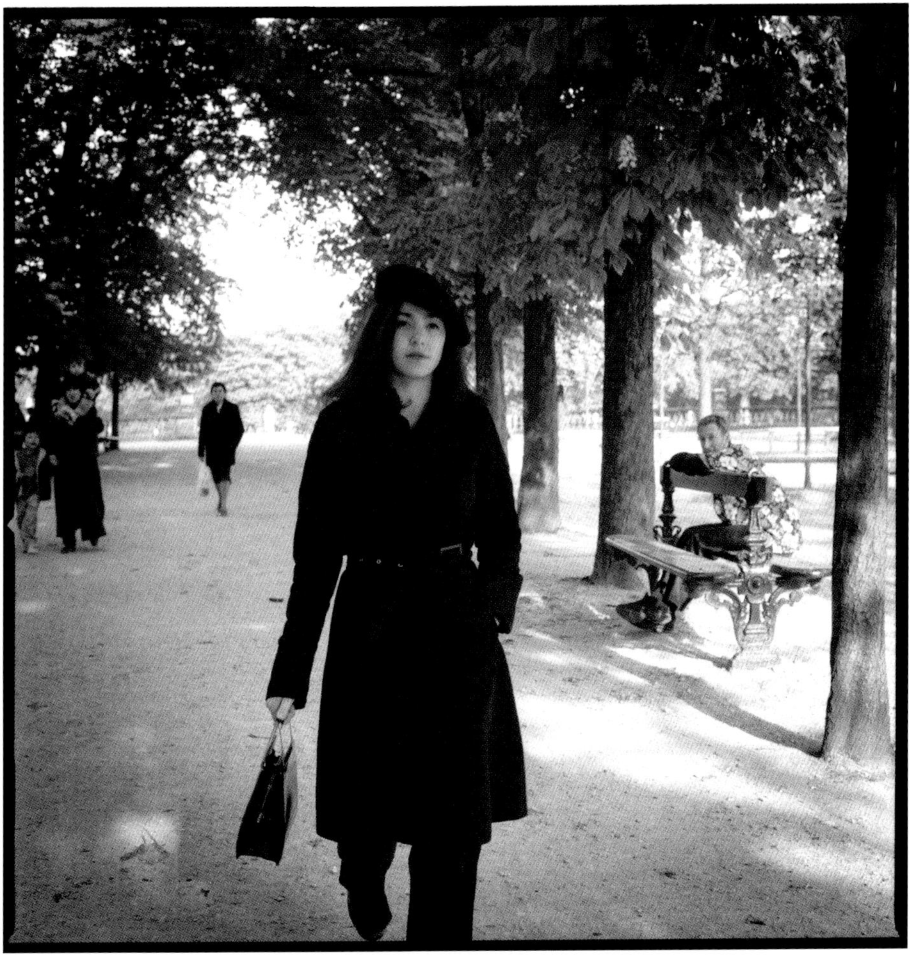

Keep dreaming!

the best hairdressers

Personalized cuts for the uniqueness of every head.

L'Atelier de Donato

If you get inspired to sharpen your image during a shopping spree, spoil yourself to a cool haircut before purchasing an armload of quality hair products from Colette's across the street. From 30 euros for juniors to 153 euros for a cut with highlights.

207, rue St Honoré 75001 Paris
Tel : 01 40 20 45 18

Dessange International

Go strait to Madeleine Cofano's private salon. Don't forget to make an appointment.

43, Avenue Franklin D.-Roosevelt 75008 Paris
Tel : 01 43 59 31 31

Charlie en Particulier

A must. The style-research consultation costs 200 euros. Here, get yourself a gorgeous haircut, the last accessory to go with your new chic outfit. Look like a Hollywood star drifting through Paris!

1, rue Goethe, 75016 Paris
Tel : 01 47 20 94 01

Thierry Lothman

The salon where you can immortalize your new look with a photography session.

13, rue Etienne Marcel 75001 Paris
Tel : 01 43 26 06 58, 01 53 00 91 80

Only idiots never change their minds.

Fench proverb

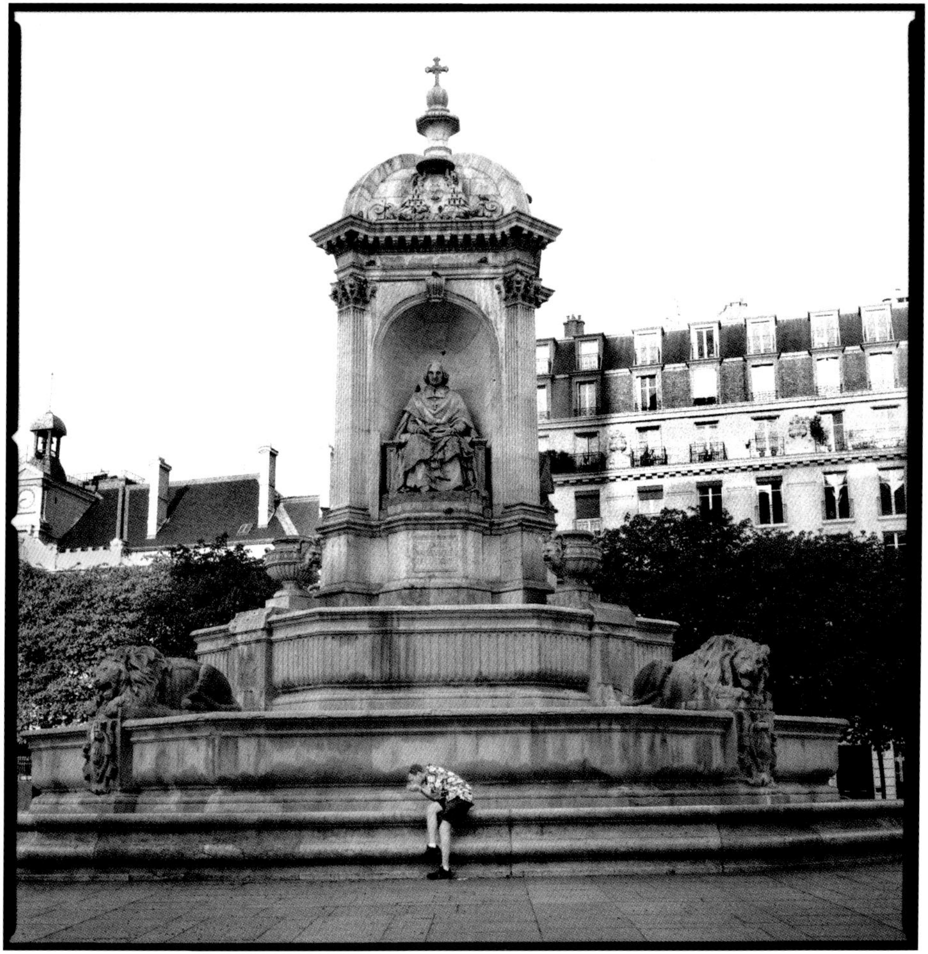

In Paris, the bottled water REALLY is preferable!

Too white a lady has a shady ass.

Fench proverb

Massato

It is needless to introduce this Japanese hairstylist and his 20-year studio career. Styles range from 85 to 185 euros.

5, rue Volney 75002 Paris
Tel : 01 42 96 10 04

Au Pays d'Oscar :

This salon is designed for children. No need to drag them there, the salon is fully equipped with cotton candy and cookies. Clients from 5 months old are welcome to come for short nips between naps. Cuts run about 24 euros for 5-year-olds.

6, rue Vavin 75006 Paris
Tel : 0826 000 616
www.oscar@wanadoo.fr

The colorists

Coloré par Rodolphe

Get colored by the master himself. From 76 euros for a dye to 230 euros for a color.

26 rue Danielle Casanova
Tel : 01 42 61 46 59

Colorist Christophe Robin

The luxury of fabulous color is expensive, but Christophe makes every penny is worth it. From 275 to 400 euros.

7, rue du Mont Thabor 75001 Paris
Tel : 01 42 60 99 15

5 rue Alger 75001 Paris
01 40 20 92 12

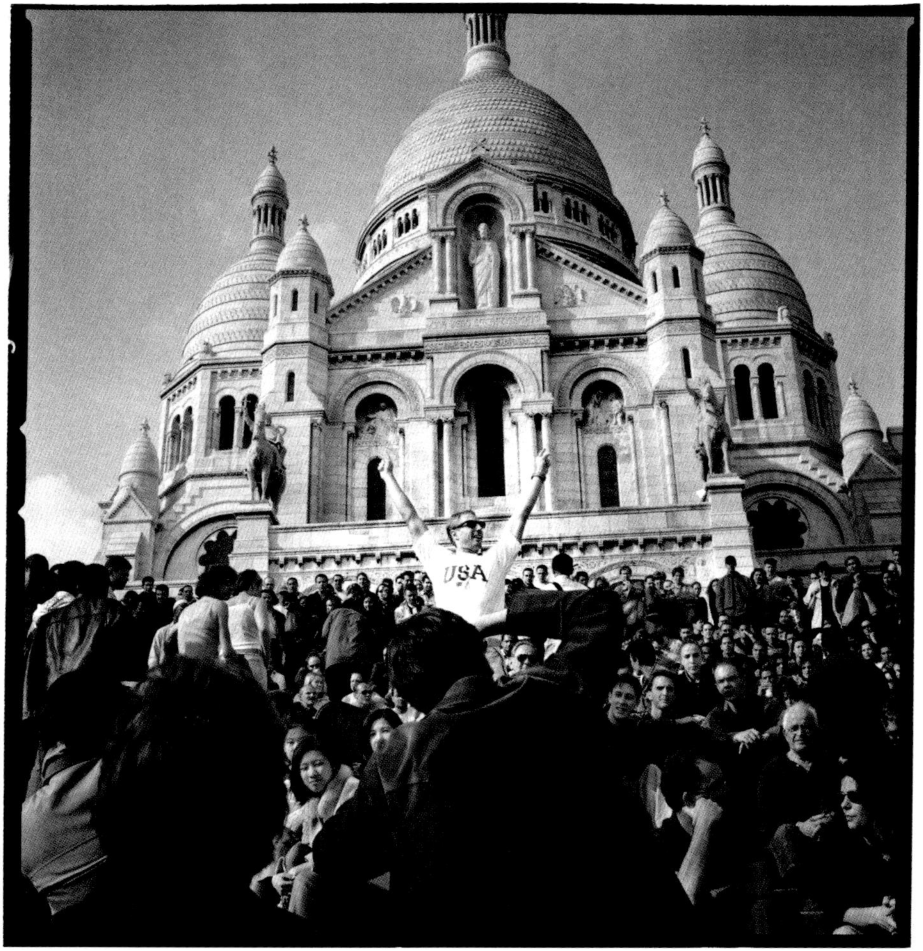

Be cool, not a fool!

Lovers always have one eye on the fields and the other on the city.

Fench proverb, by Montluc

Treat your hair to something special

Vog

Keep your hair healthy and shiny! Vog offers anti-stress treatments, fig and ginger cataplasms, and more… From 30 to 60 euros.

416, rue St Honoré 75008 Paris
Tel : 01 42 86 84 33
www.vog.fr

Léonor Greyl

Orchid masks, precious oils and flower based creams. 70 euros per hair treatment.

15 rue Tronchet 75008 Paris
Tel : 01 42 65 32 26
www.leonorgreyl.com

New Parisian Global Beauty d'Alexandre Zouari

Another name that will make your hair tingle with pleasure. Get a cut and styling for 85 euros. You can also indulge in a manicure for 23 euros, and a facial for 70 euros.

1, avenue du Président Wilson 75016 Paris
Tel : 01 47 23 79 00
www.alexandre-zouari.com

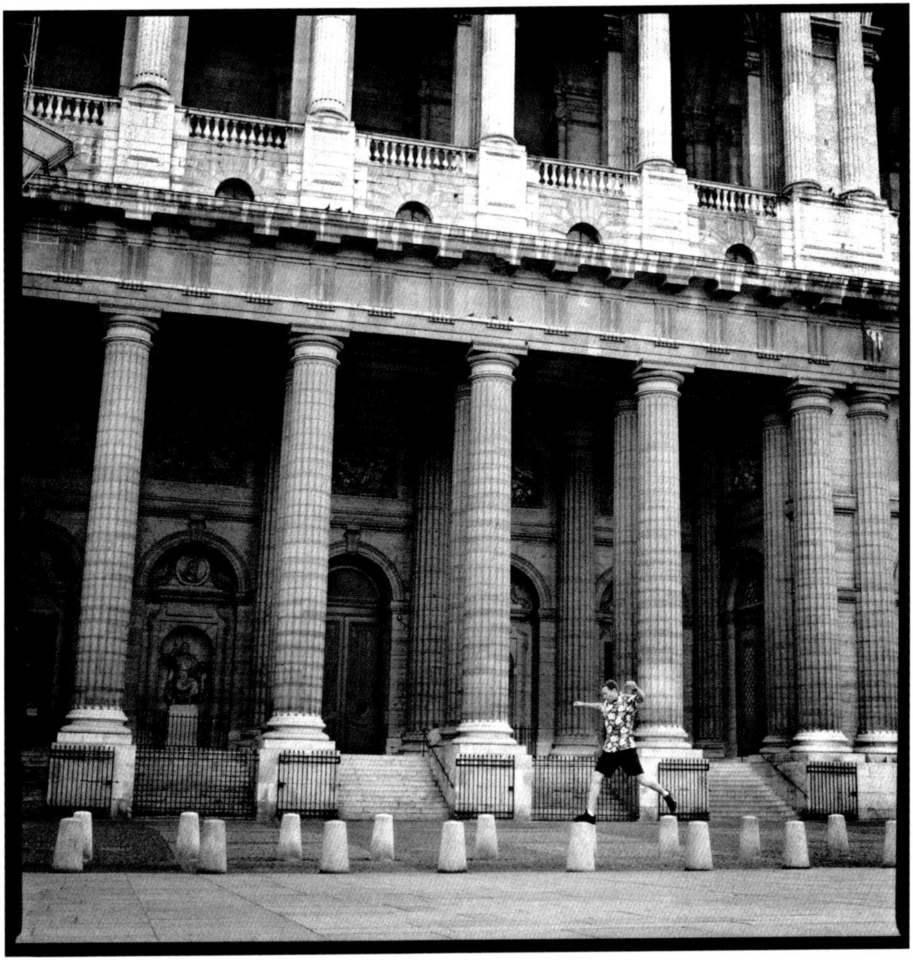

The grandeur of Paris leaves you walking on air

Personal trainers that make house calls

Personalized Gym:

Bruno Fuscien-Trasan, a trainer at the Ritz Health Club, offers personalized sessions to fit your schedule and objectives. Prices : 70 euros per hour, 100 euros for two.

Tel : 06 10 74 22 87

Personal trainer

Get a one-on-one training session with a personal trainer who comes to your doorsteps.

Tel: 06 85 13 48 73 - Craig

Personal Coach

To get back in shape, lose weight and look great, find a motivating coach. Francois Verdier recommended.

Tel: 06 21 32 54 54

Stretching-Dance-Personal Trainer

All in one. Anabelle Baranes recommended.

Tel: 06 16 93 49 12

Sport Pilates

Get that toner, well-balanced, stronger body with pilates. Benefits: assisting in aligning the body, increase energy levels, stretches and strengthens the body, a great work out for the abdominals, ideal for healthy weight loss and general well-being. Just opened, considered the best in Paris.

12, rue de la Neva 75008 Paris
Tel: 01 43 80 66 36

Body sculpting :

Jérôme Vincienne offers lessons in weight loss and toning. He's also a state-certified French kickboxing instructor and can initiate you in self-defense. Prices: 53 euros per hour for 10 lessons.

Tel : 01 53 32 50 44 and 06 61 58 90 00

When you're alone, you become necessary.

Fench proverb

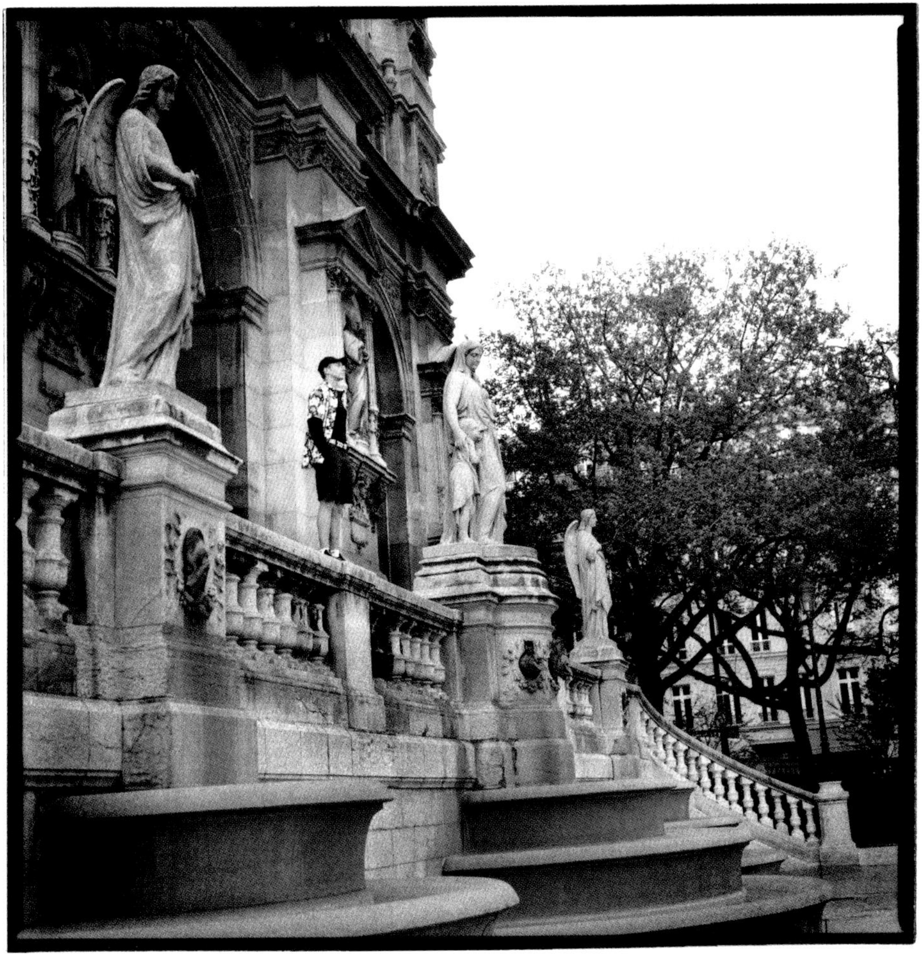

O, sweet angels...

Every frog finds it's toad.

Fench proverb

Yoga forever :

Arnaud Zemb will send you to nirvana, for those of you who haven't been, thanks to Ashtanga Yoga. Prices: 70 euros per hour at your home, 50 euros at his place.

Tel : 06 21 03 56 27

Massage

Olivier Lecocq. A specialist in Chinese massage and shiatsu, this masseur was certified at the School of Chinese Acupuncture in Paris and works in the grand hotels or at home. Suggested: foot massages (reflexology) or energetic full body massage inspired by shiatsu. From 32 to 115 euros an hour.

54 Boulevard du Temple 750011 Paris

Tel : 06 10 15 02 51

www.monmasseur.com

A relaxologist

A specialist in stress management, **Nadine Fleizman** is a trained relaxologist. She offers lessons in light gym, tai chi, relaxation and stretching.

Prices : 68 euros per hour, 77 euros for two.

Tel : 06 14 71 05 78

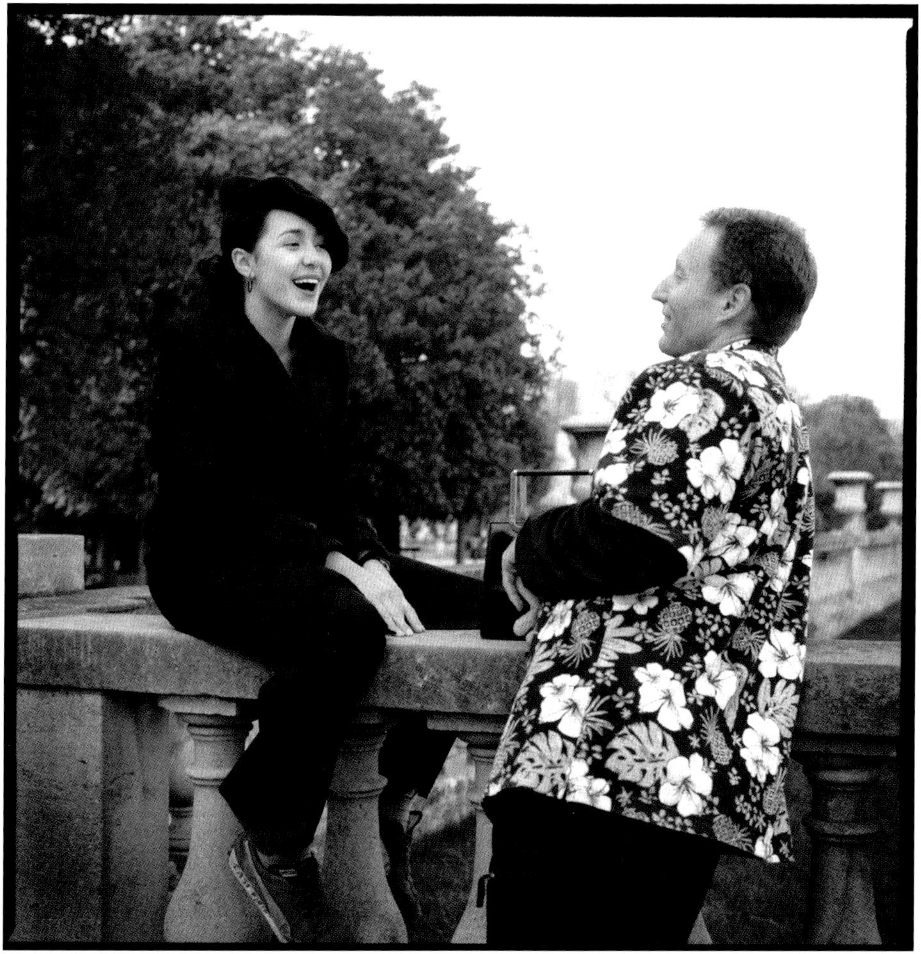

suit yourself, Hawaiian shirts are chic back home.

Little gifts maintain a friendship.

Fench proverb

Cent Dessus Dessous

We all know that Paris remains the capital of glamour, all things sexy, and of course, lingerie. So, what better place to get an overdose on it? Subject yourself to a little sin and be the object of desire. Use your man's credit card and go crazy, he too will enjoy. The things we do in the name of love!

305 rue St. Jacques 75005 Paris
Tel: 01 43 54 02 36

Fifi Chachnill

Yes, you got the name right. No, it's not a revised Kama Sutra position. It's the name of the creator of this 19th Century style boudoir with floating veils, and silks and embroidery used to make dresses and skirts that are all short enough you earn you a good spanking. Buyer beware!

68 rue Jean Jacques Rousseau 75001 Paris
Tel: 01 42 21 19 93

Sabbia Rosa

The Parisian lingerie institution. Dreams and fantasies guaranteed.

73, rue des St Pères 75006 Paris
Tel : 01 45 48 88 37

shopping

He who accepts a gift loses his liberty.

Slavic proverb

Les Nuits de Satin

In the heart of the St Ouen flea market, these two specialized shops orffer corset from 1900s and collections of lingerie and accessories from the 50s and 60s. These jewels, never worn, are sold in their original packaging.

Marché Dauphine
140, rue des Rosiers
93400 St Ouen 2nd floor stands198 and 284
Tel : 06 09 91 32 30

9 rue Oberkampf 75011 Paris
Tel: 01 43 57 65 05

Princesse Tam Tam

The best value in a variety of lingerie – provocative, romantic, innocent, playful... It's enough to satisfy the bulimic urges of all you urban princesses.

20, rue St Antoine 75004 Paris
Tel : 01 42 77 32 27
www.princessetamtam.com

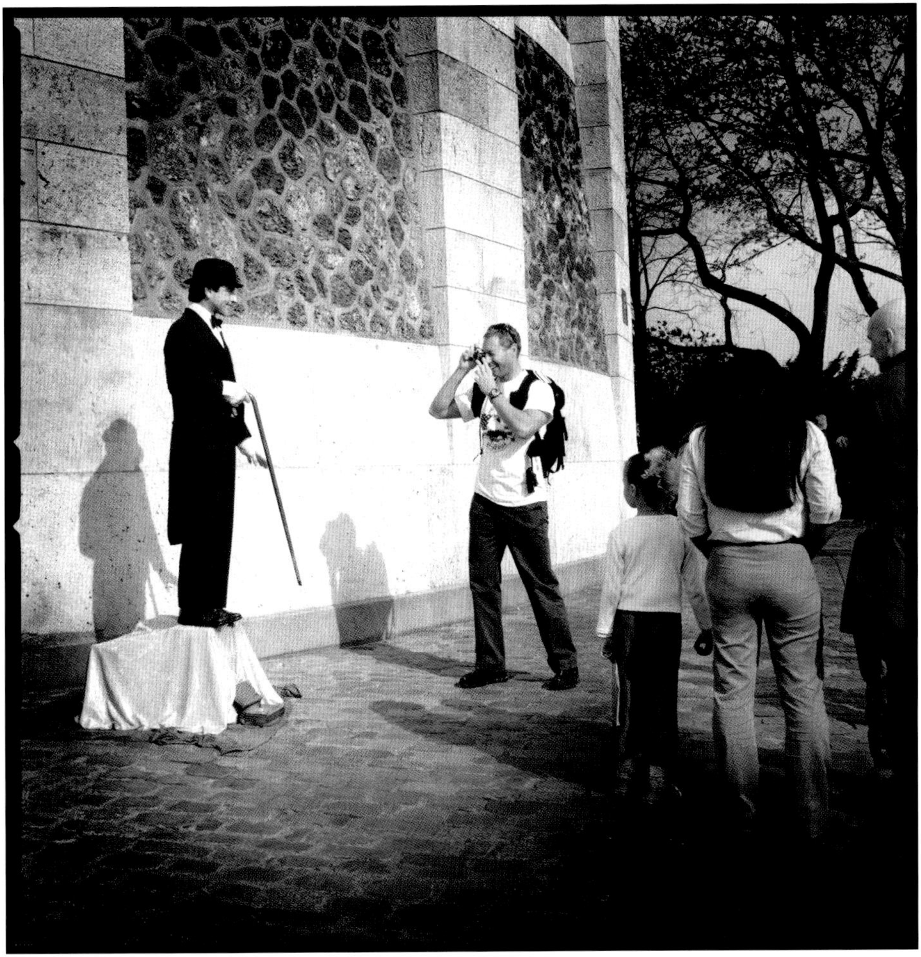

The city of lights and entertainement ... don't forget to tip.

You can dress a hedgehog to look like a baron.

Fench proverb

Surprise! - Ohhhh, you shouldn't have!

The best florists

Vertumme

Clarisse Beraud's creations are about spontaneity, colors and freshness.

12, rue de la Sourdière 75001 Paris
Tel : 01 42 86 06 76
atelier.vertumne@wanadoo.fr

Christian Tortu

For the past 15 years, Tortu is the name representing a revolution in the art of the bouquet.

6, carrefour de l'Odéon 75006 Paris
Tel : 01 43 26 02 56

Ryu Kubota

The only ikebana specialist in Paris

40, Bd Raspail 75007 Paris
Tel : 01 45 48 00 98

Paris and Fashion – don't hesitate to splurge in the world's fashion center, but go with someone who has an eye for style. Otherwise, Parisian retail shrews, who attach so much importance to a material goods, might work you into looking like an Austin Powers fashionista

Colette

All the latest trends, at a few steps ahead of the competition.

213, rue St Honoré 75001 Paris
Tel : 01 55 35 33 90
www.colette.f

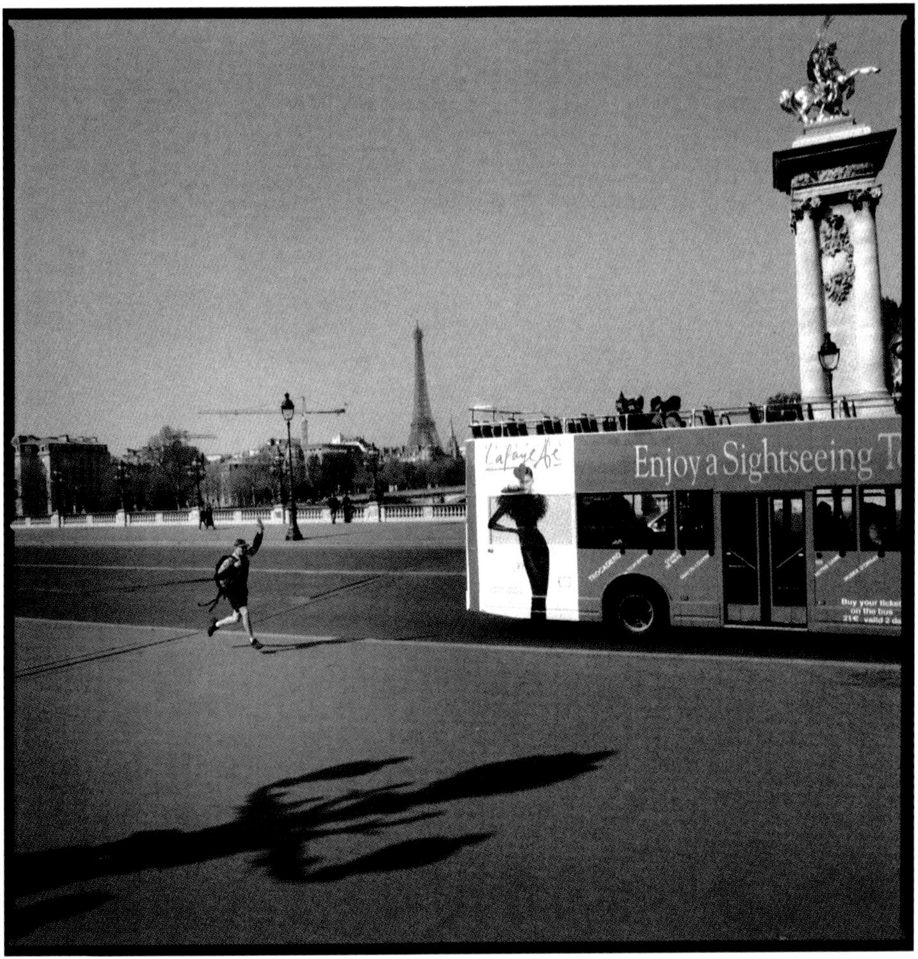

Don't miss the tour buses,
it's a long walk around town.

Between skin and shirt, you need to hide the good that you do.

Fench proverb, by La Fontaine

L'Eclaireur

The Parisian pioneer Armand Hadida follows the world's biggest creators very closely to offer a good selection of their works of art.

10, rue Hérold 75001 Paris
Tel : 01 40 41 09 89

3 ter rue des Rosiers 75004 Paris
Tel : 01 48 87 10 22

29 rue de Valois 75001 Paris
Tel: 01 40 20 42 52

12 rue de Malher 75004 Paris
Tel: 01 44 54 22 11

Rag et Vertiges

Going with the flow of vintage trends, here you will find a collection of clothing belonging to several groovy decades from the 40s through the 70s. All at very affordable prices.

83-85, rue St Martin 75003 Paris
Tel : 01 48 87 34 64

fashion

A happy man has no shirt.

Fench proverb

Antik Batik

A style that take Indian trends to a new and exciting height. You will absolutely fall in love with this store!

18, rue de Turenne 75004 Paris
Tel : 01 44 78 02 00

38, rue Vaigirard 75006 Paris
Tel: 01 43 25 30 22
www.antikbatik.fr

Xuly Bët

The King of Funky Fashion. After shopping here, go straight to a nightclub.

1 rue Pierre Lescot 75004 Paris
Tel: 01 42 33 50 40

104, rue Folie Mericourt 75011 Paris
Tel: 01 47 00 02 09

Vanessa Bruno

This former model made herself a star in Japan with her "glam rock" look. A must-see shop for all the fashion victims out their.

25, rue St Sulpice 75006 Paris
Tel : 01 43 54 41 04

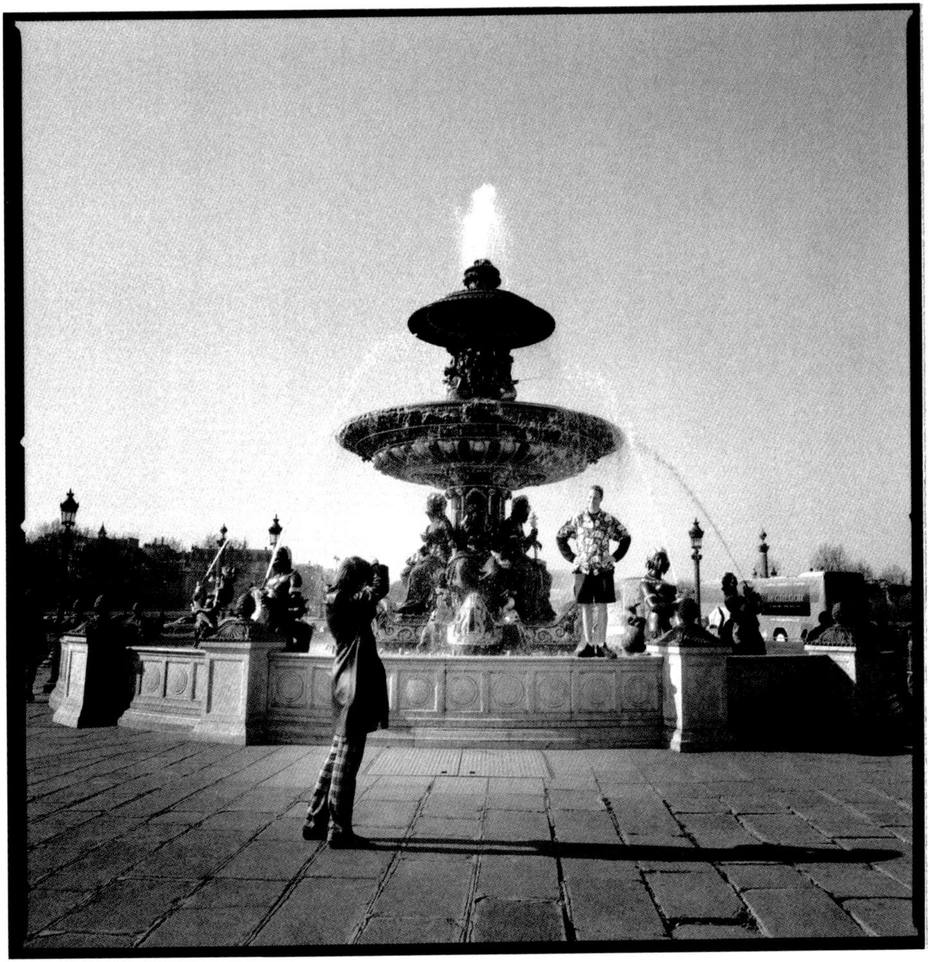

Feel free to pose like a fountain when next to a fountain

While waiting for the shoes of the dead, you may stay barefoot for some time.

Fench proverb, by Le Bourbonnais

APC Surplus

Introduce this store to your friends in secret code. This is the IT place to find all the great goodies that big stores don't carry. Very reasonably priced. A crying shame to miss!

45, rue Madame 75006 Paris
Tel : 01 45 48 43 71

Isabel Marant

For girls with ambitions to be the new Parisian icon of glamour.

16 rue de Charonne 75011 Paris
Tel: 01 49 29 71 55

Guerrisold

This unavoidable address is the last stop of your initiation. After going to Gerrisold, you can show off your shocking Parisian chic side. In the Barbès district, this boutique offers a medley of clothing and accessories, ranging from the total piece of crap, to the pearl of fashion for a few euros.

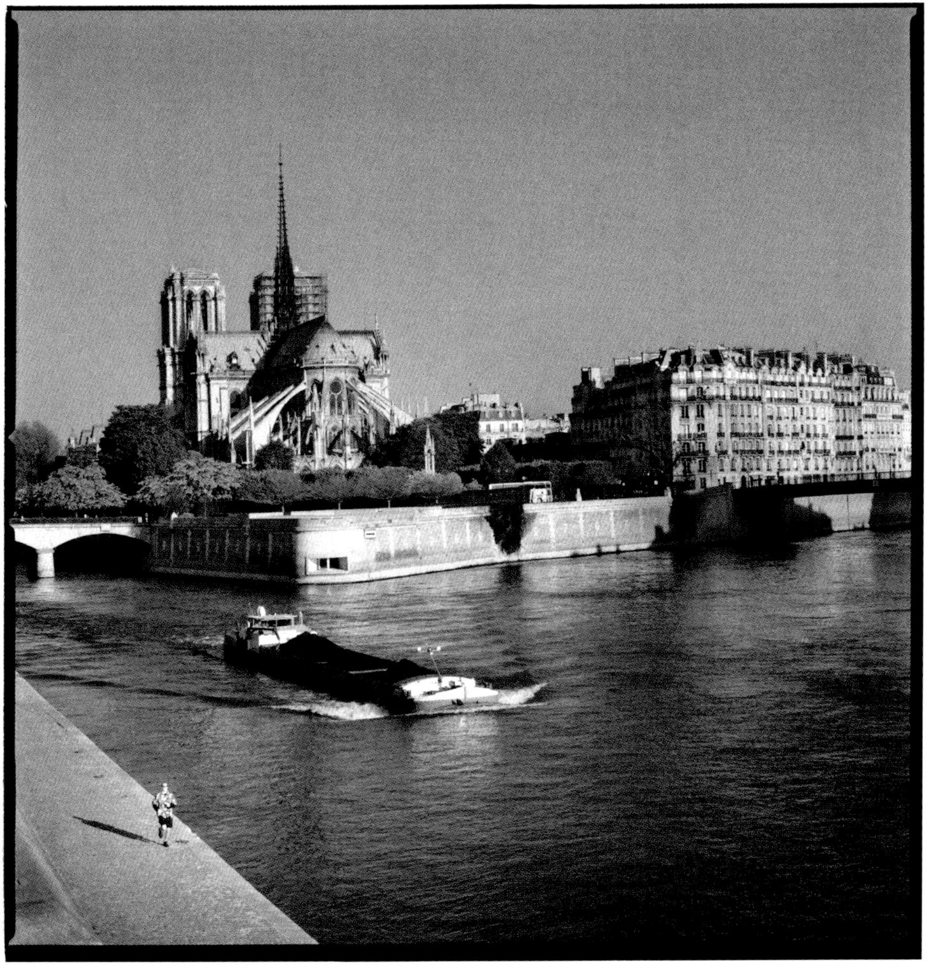

when you gotta go, you gotta go ... !!!

What about shoes?

ATTENTION: Self-confessed shoe-whores! This is your vital list of where to find the most beautiful shoes in Paris, if not the world. Send those Italians back to the drawing board...

Rodolphe Ménudier

The fashion critics' all-around favorite.

14, rue de Castiglione 75001 Paris
Tel : 01 42 60 86 27

Michel Perry

For a snazzy touch of Rock 'n' Roll.

243, rue St. Honore 75001 Paris
Tel : 01 42 44 10 07

It's better to be envied than pitied.

Fench proverb

Christian Louboutin

Simply Number One! Hand-sewn and all.

38, rue de Grenelle 75007 Paris
Tel: 01 42 22 33 07

Facteur Céleste

Designed and made by African and Asian women, the shoes here have a hint of various cultures around the world. Also keep a lookout for other treasures.

38, rue Quincampoix 75004 Paris
Tel: 01 42 77 12 46

art & culture

Musée du Louvre

o see it all, you'd have to camp out… The Louvre has one of the world's largest art collections. If you don't have five weeks to see all 65,300 masterpieces, first check out the three most famous ones – the Mona Lisa, Venus de Milo and Winged Victory. Built in 1190 by King Phillippe Auguste to protect Paris from the Vikings, this enormous horseshoe-shaped building was once a fortress. The Louvre is the longest building in Europe, stretching farther than three times the length of the Eiffel Tower measured from end to end. Take a stroll around Louvre's entire perimeter, if you can handle the awesome three-mile challenge! In 1989, the Pritzker Prize honoree Ieoh Ming Pei designed the dazzling 71-foot tall glass pyramid, made of exactly 666 panes, for the museum's Renaissance courtyard. It is a neomodern structure is attached to much controversy. Admission tickets range from 6 to 54 euros, depending on your schedule. Museum passes available for consecutive-day visits: 1 day (18 euros), 3 says (36 euros), 5 days (54 euros).

Palais Royal 75001 Paris

Tel : 01 40 20 53 17

www.louvre.fr

The nuts create trends, and the wise follow them.

Fench proverb

Musée d'Orsay

Good collections of art from 1848 to 1914.
The newly reopened entrance facilities and auditorium allow rich programs of exhibitions, concerts, shows, film festivals, etc. The Musee d'Orsay houses permanent exhibitions of 4,000 artworks in about 80 separate galleries. Enjoy coffee between exhibitions in the Café des Hauteurs on the 5th floor. Or, do lunch at the Musée d'Orsay Restaurant, situated in what used to be the restaurant of the Gare d'Orsay hotel. Its turn of the 19th Century décor offers a relaxing setting for a break on your visit. The d'Orsay Bookshop offers 6,000 titles on painting, sculpture, architecture, decorative arts, French and foreign museum collections, photography, and children's books. Buy souvenirs at The Boutique, where you'll find great gift ideas and jewelry. The Postcard Shop carries a large selection of postcards and other media goods as well as a special range of stationery. Consecutive-day museum passes: 1 day (18 euros), 3 days (36 euros), 5 days (54 euros).

62, rue de Lille 75007 Paris

Tel : 01 40 49 48 14

www.musee-orsay.fr

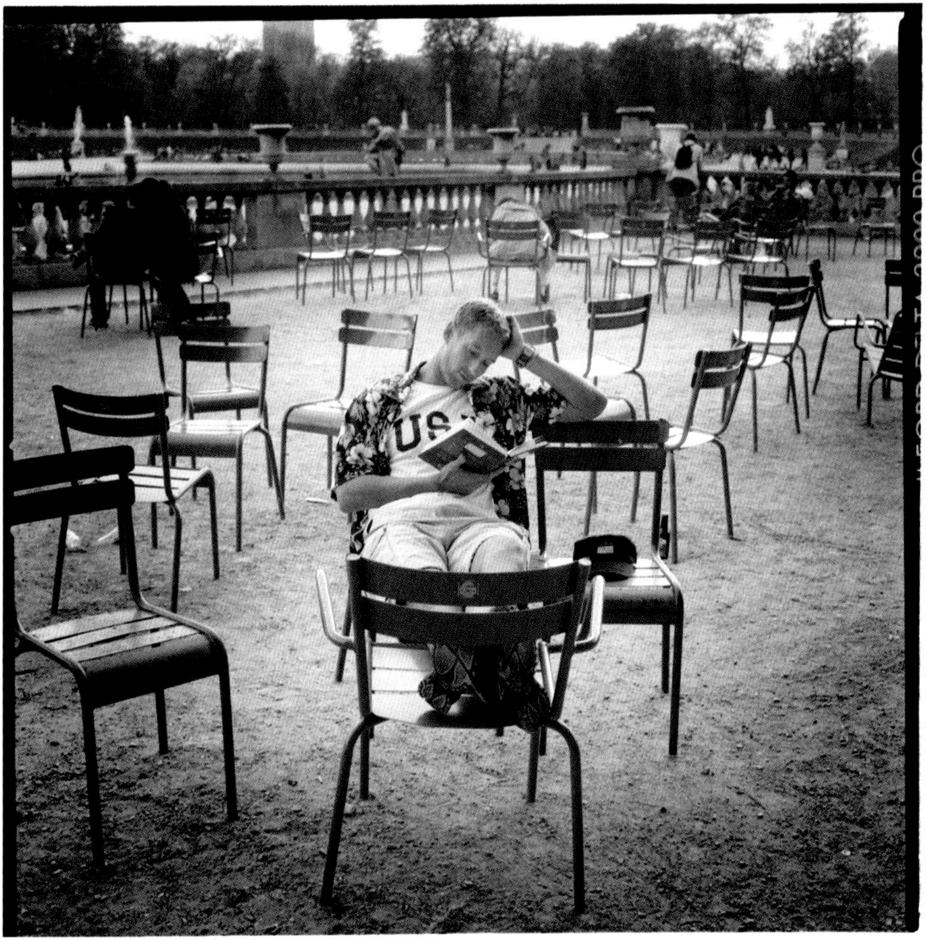

Every hectic city has a quiet spot...

The parks around Paris are great instant gateways.

A wise person knows how to be nuts.

Fench proverb

Centre Georges Pompidou

Situated in the heart of Paris, the Pompidou is one of the most important cultural institutions in the world, and representative of the Parisian modern art museum. Symbolizing the spirit of the 20th Century, the architecture of the Pompidou was designed by famous visionaries Richard Rogers, Renzo, Piano and Gianfranco Franchini. The goal was to meet the criterion of interdisciplinary, freedom of movement and an open approach to exhibition areas. The Pompidou Center first opened to the public in 1977 and since 2000 it has become one of the most frequently visited monuments in France. In a unique location under a single roof, the center houses the leading collections of contemporary art in Europe, a vast public reference library with over 2,000 places to work, general documentation on 20th Century art, cinema and performance halls, an institute for musical research, educational activity areas, bookshops, a restaurant and a café. Tickets are 10 euros.

19 rue Beaubourg 75004 Paris
Tel : 01 44 78 12 33
www.centrepompidou.fr

Musée de l'Erotisme

If you didn't have the courage to visit the three art monsters mentioned above, at least go see this one. Exhibitions: Rated R, or above. This is the artsy version of Boulevard de Clichy (the main street of the Pigalle district). If you need to find a sex shop, there's one a few doors down called "Baisodrome" (French for "orgy"). Need we say more?

72, Bd de Clichy 75018 Paris
Tel : 01 42 58 28 73

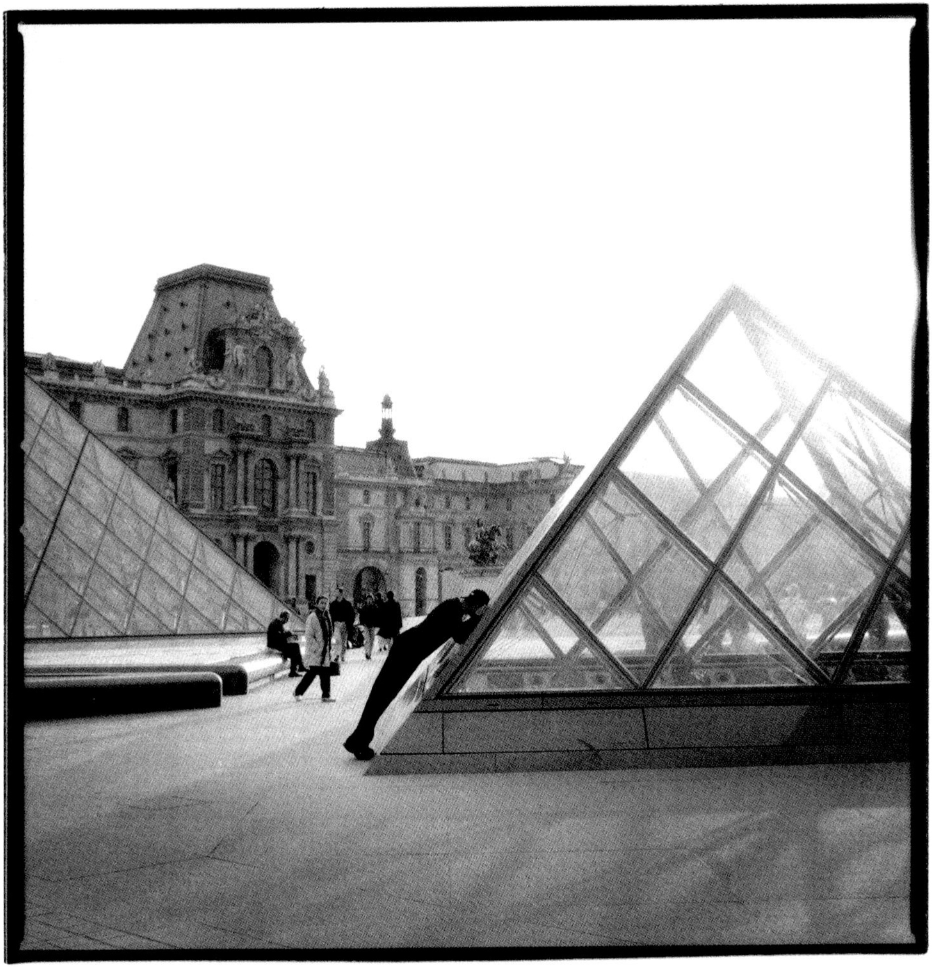

You can't see the Mona Lisa from here.
Just buy a ticket to the Louvre

The finer of the two is not the one who sings, but the one who listens.

Fench proverb, from Agen

Galerie Daniel Templon

Highly concentrated on Contemporary Art. Features: Arman, Jean Michel Alberola, Claude Viallat, the Chapman brothers, Jean Michel Basquiat, Martin Barré, Daniel Buren, Oliver Debré, Jean-Marc Bustamente.

30, rue Beaubourg 75003 Paris
Tel : 01 42 72 14 10

Galerie Thaddaeus Ropac

"Unavoidable gallery of work by the most prestigious visionary artists in the last century. Doesn't that say more than enough? Features: : Georg Baselitz, Dobald Baechler, Wolfgang Laib, Tom Sachs, Jeff Koons.

7, rue Debelleyme 75003 Paris
Tel : 01 42 72 99 00
www.ropac.net

Galerie Pierre Brullé

If you're not sure about the difference between Kandinski and kindergarten modern art, this place will straighten you out. If you're a self-proclaimed art guru, come here knowing that your art knowledge will be tested, to say the least. Pierre Brulle isn't overly concerned about the art market, he exhibits stuff he likes such as pieces of a precious edition. Chosen by a golden eye… you'll be shaken, not stirred!

25, rue de Tournon 75006 Paris
Tel : 01 43 25 18 73

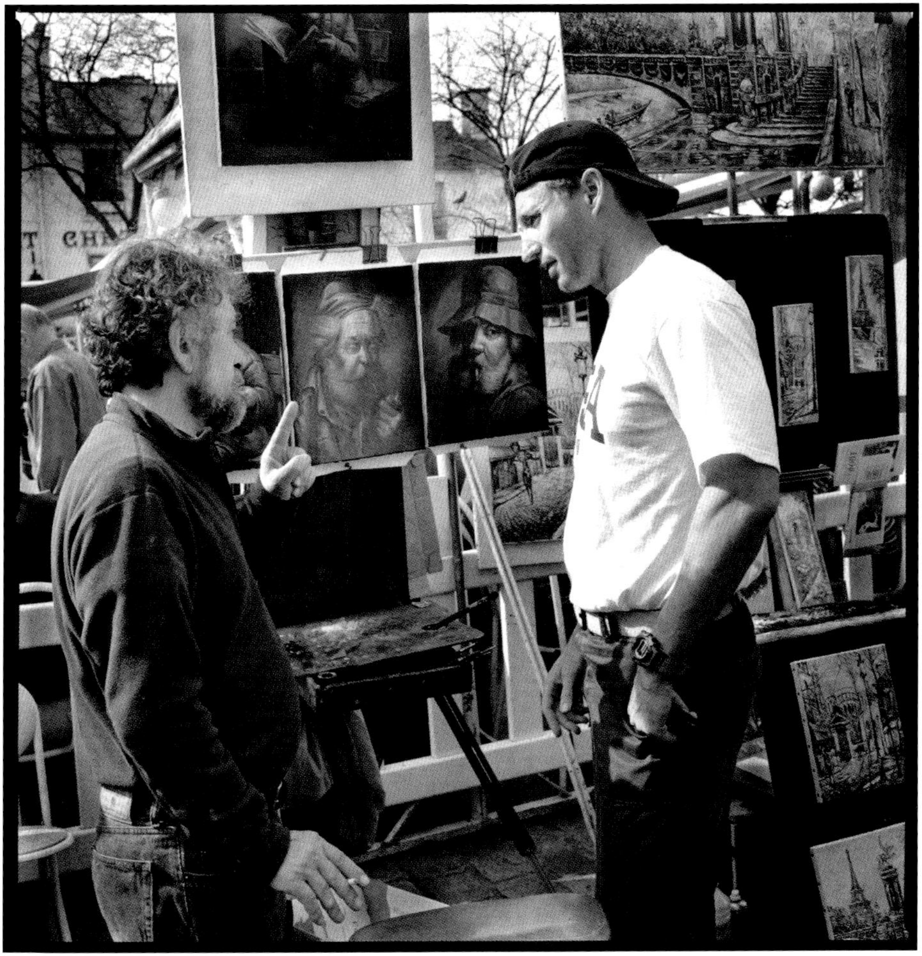

Montmartre is a great place to pick up a painting, but you probably won't find any Grateful Dead posters!

The art is to hide the art.

Fench proverb

Galerie Seine 51

A nice place to start for Americans in Paris. You'll feel at home here with Pop Art and Neo-Realism on your agenda. The first will help you prepare for the second. Features:

51, rue de Seine 75006 Paris
Tel : 01 43 26 91 10

Galerie Lelong

From the primitive art of Wilfredo Lam to Michaux, Pagès, Saura, Ernest Pignon-Ernest.

13, rue de Téhéran 75008 Paris
Tel : 01 45 63 13 19

Fondation Cartier

If you're still not yet ecstatic about Parisian culture, go here. No need to be artsy-fartsy. This is an entire different culture… from the South Pacific. In this elegant establishment, known for its exceptional quality and beauty, you'll find a rich culture of pearls, a timeless and tasteful kind of art with a special purpose. jousts and bazaar art.

261, Bd Raspail 75014 Paris
Tel : 01 42 18 56 50
www.fondation.cartier.fr

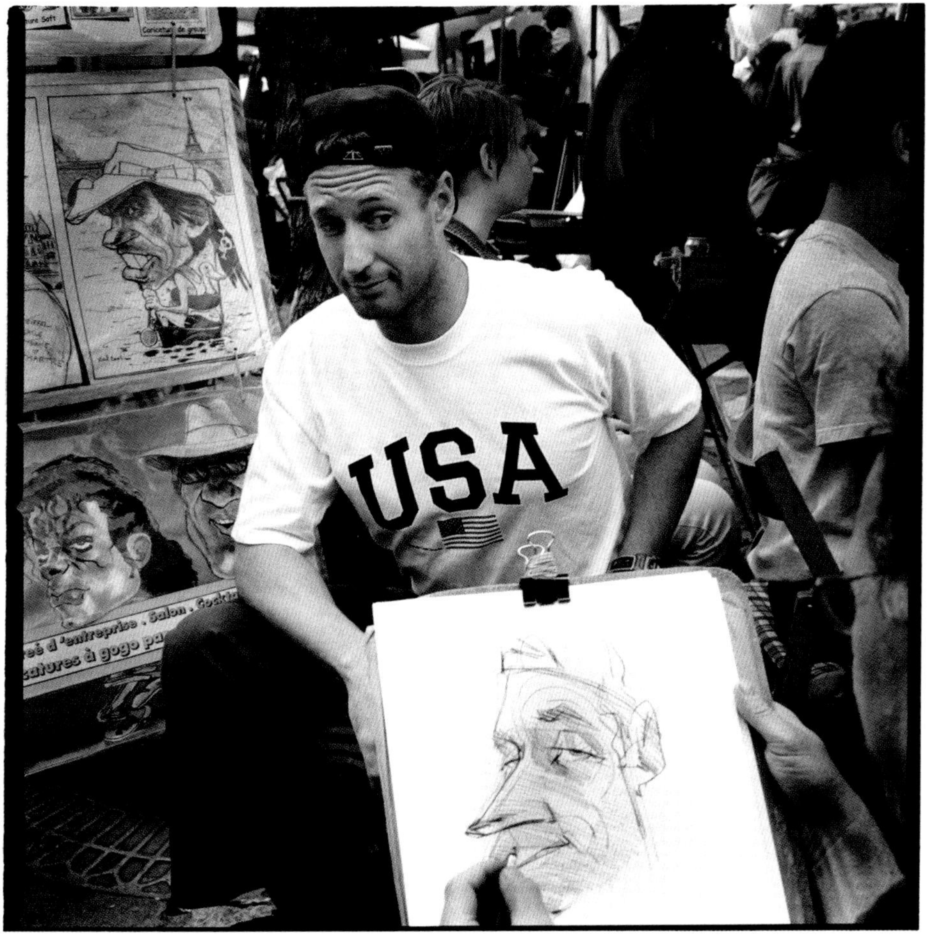

is that your mustache or mine ... ?

No one should be asked the impossible.

Fench proverb

Maison de la culture du Japon

A great place for you cravers of Japanese comics and the work of Yayoi Kusama. Features a sharp presentation of Japan's ultra avant-garde art. You'll discover the unique evolution of Japanese society. If you prefer the trendy Zen sensation, come to the tea ceremonies on Wednesdays. Reservations recommended.

101 bis Quai Branly 75015 Paris
Tel : 01 44 37 95 01
www.mcjp.asso.fr

JMG Galerie

Here, art giants await you – Tom Wesselmann, Niki St. Phalle, Marina Karella, Cesar, Igor Midoraj, Jean Tinguely, Takis.

79, rue du Temple 75011 Paris
Tel : 01 43 26 12 05
www.jgmgalerie.com

Photographs

Galerie Agathe Gaillard

Agathe Gaillard opened Paris' first photo gallery in 1975.
The quality of the photography exhibited here is flawless. Photo geniuses featured include: Cartier Bresson, Edgerton, Boubat, Riboud, Mme Yevonde.

3, rue du Pont Louis-Philippe 75004 Paris
Tel : 01 42 77 38 24

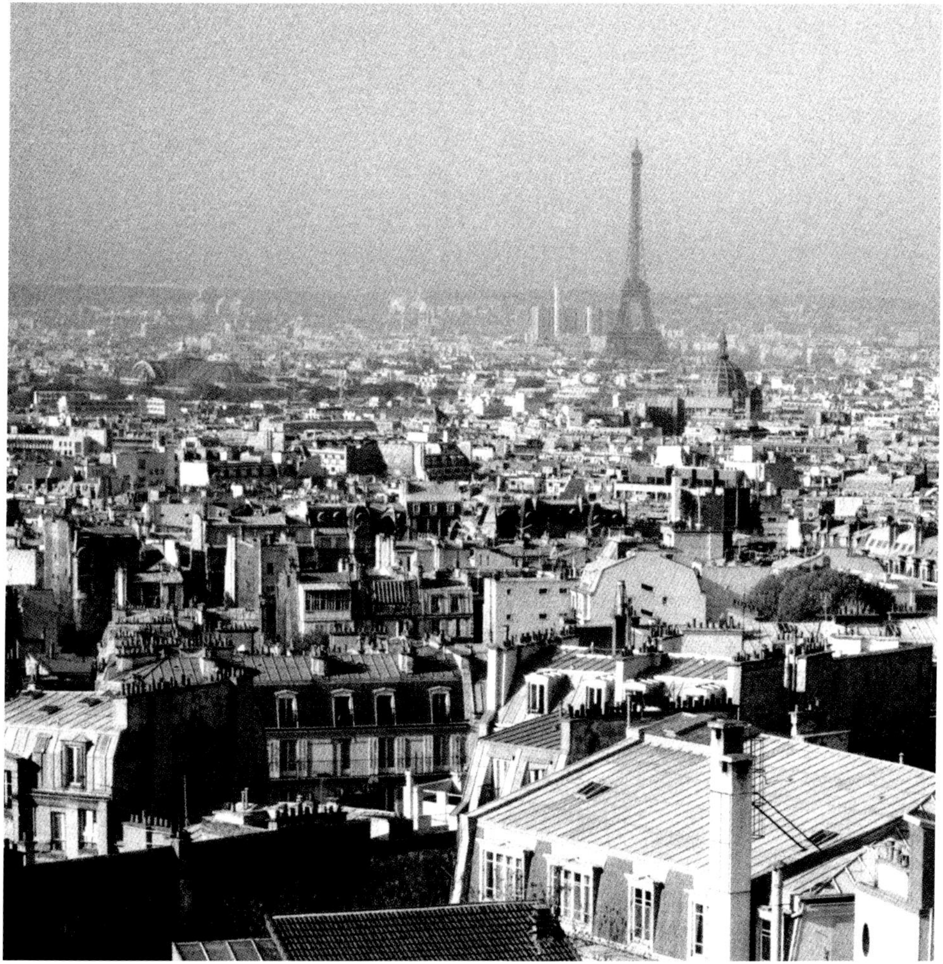

yes the maps are in French too!

Galerie Vu

The six expositions held annually are organized by Christian Caujeolle, a prominent figure in photography and curator of Vu. Featured are: Laurence Leblanc, Juan Manuel, Castro, Prieto, Cristina Garcia Rodero, Hiroto Fujimoto, Jeh-Song Baak, Anders Peterson.

2, rue Jules Cousin 75002 Paris
Tel : 01 53 01 85 81
www.agencevu.com

Hôtel de Sully

Since 1994, the walls of the exposition rooms in this hotel have been home to the Patrimoine Photographique, an association that conserves and distributes state collections. With millions of prints to constitute one grand collection of 20th Century masters, it features Andre Kertesz, Sam Levin, Denise Colomb and many others

62, rue St Antoine 75004 Paris
Tel : 01 44 61 20 00
www.monum.fr

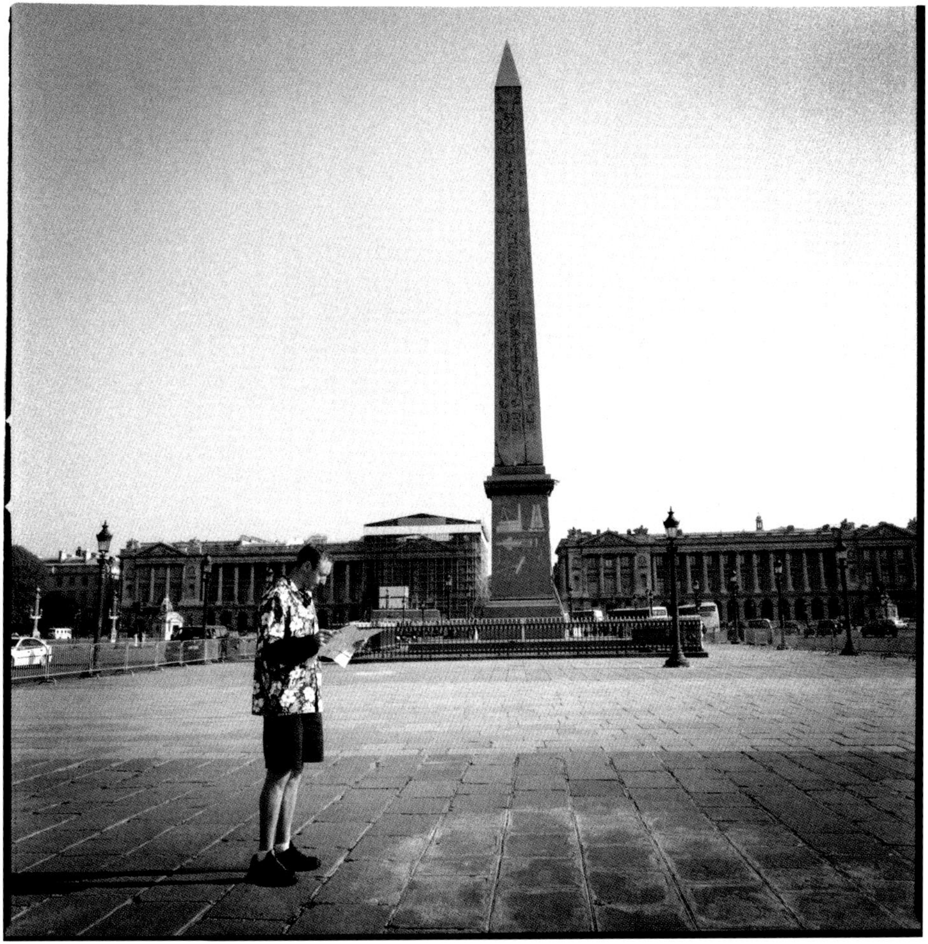

Sightseeing in Paris can be great if you remember to look up every now and then!

Maison Européenne de la Photographie

Enjoy losing your way through 27,000 square feet dedicated solely to photography. This maison is the richest photography library in Paris

5-7, rue de Fourcy 75004 Paris
Tel : 01 44 78 75 00
www.mep-fr.org

Centre National de la Photographie

Run by the Ministry of Culture, this establishment is known for giving young artists from around the world their first break. An excellent place to see something out of the ordinary.

Hôtel Salomon de Rothschild, 11, rue Berryer 75008 Paris
Tel : 01 53 76 12 32

...and

for the very lazy...books in English.

American Library

10 rue de General Camou 75007 Paris
Tel : 01 53 59 12 60
www.americanlibraryinparis.com

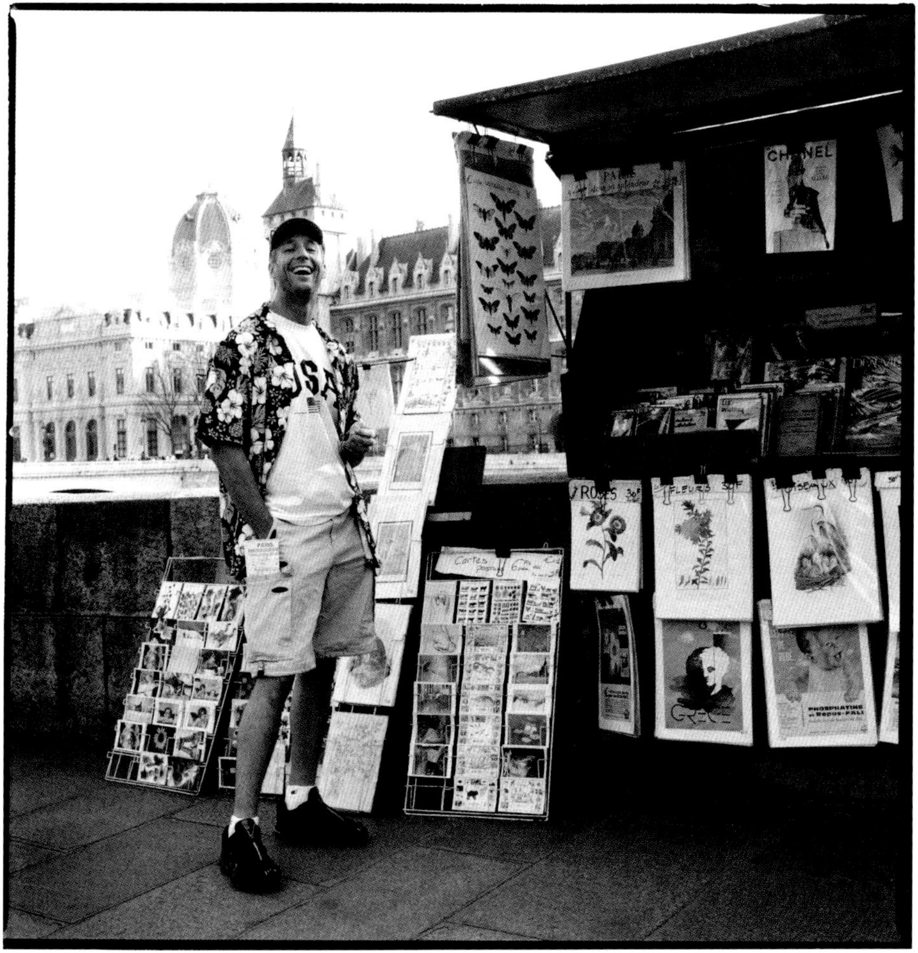

Dressed appropriately, you can blend in really well!!!

Acknowledgments

This book would not have been possible without the help of all my
Parisians friends, whom I would like to thank personally:
Laurence Delesti
Grégoire Malher
Leila Smara
Alice Vial
Anna Wloch
Nicolas Duchemin Harvard
Nadia Hamam
Alain and Arnaud at Paris Photo Lab

A big thank you to John Riggs for being the funny American tourist!
Also to Victor Sirgado, Christine Uskevich, Joey Krutel, Cynthia Lawry, Sandy Bosem, Debra Vasquez,
Dr. Herbert P. Riggs and Robert Avellan for finding time to put this book together..

Riggs Publishing Media-www.contactrpm.com
Printed in China
ISBN: 09762988-0-5
EAN: 9780976298809
LOCN: 2004098384

design by Robert Avellan